GOD'S CHAOS
CODE

GOD'S CHAOS CODE

THE SHOCKING BLUEPRINT THAT REVEALS
5 KEYS TO THE DESTINY OF NATIONS

LANCE WALLNAU
WITH MERCEDES SPARKS

KILLER SHEEP MEDIA, INC.

This book is dedicated to my children and to their generation. You are stepping into the greatest and most momentous chapter of history since the founding of Jesus's original first-century movement; and, like them, you will do exploits.

CONTENTS

FOREWORD

BY MARIO MURILLO

When I read the manuscript of Lance Wallnau's new book, *God's Chaos Code*, I was overtaken by excitement and hope. I can count on one hand the number of books that have done that to me. You simply must get this book. Let me explain why:

Before I buy a book, I ask myself questions. What makes a book great? What makes a book a must-read? Clarity is a key part. Does the book clear away cobwebs of confusion? In a great book, the reader doesn't work hard to figure out what the writer is trying to say.

Another component is information that is convincing. Does the book inform you with facts that leave no doubt? Does it make its case?

Another factor in a must-read book is urgency—urgency that leads to action—clear and undeniable action.

A final part of a classic book is inspiration. Is it a word from God that you can hang your life on? Did the book summon you to a level of faith and commitment you never realized you could own?

Any one of these elements, by themselves, can make a book essential, but it is rare when all of them come together in one book. That has happened in Lance Wallnau's new book, *God's Chaos Code*.

Lance declares in one sentence—let alone the rest of the book—the catalyst to a great, worldwide reformation. He sees that America is in chaos. He says since God has given us the code, we can understand why this is all happening. We can exploit the crisis itself.

We did not properly seize the gift of Donald Trump's first term. We did not build what God wanted us to build. We did not see the vast provision and direction that had been kept ready for those who would build God's house instead of their private kingdoms.

We didn't see the grandeur and majesty of the real people of God—people capable of influence that is unimaginable to the rank-and-file believer and preacher who shuttle in and out of status-quo religion.

Not only is this book essential, it is something quite unique. It is a weapon. In 1 Chronicles 12 we see the account of David's army forming. They came and brought their courage and skill for war with them. Each tribe's weaponry is detailed. Then we see a wonderful weapon in verse 32: "Of the sons of Issachar who had understanding of the times, to know what Israel ought to do ..."[1]

This book is a weapon that reveals the times we are in and tells us what God wants us to do. This is a weapon that can shift the war in our favor—that will deliver you from living below your destiny and place you squarely in the middle of God's unfolding global miracle.

—Mario Murillo

---

1 1 Chronicles 12:32 (KJV).

ACKNOWLEDGMENT

To my wife Annabelle, who has been at the
center of this adventure for thirty-five years.
I could not imagine a more perfect partner.

INTRODUCTION

HIDDEN CODES

"People do not read Introductions."
—*Lance Wallnau*

Y ou must be different than most people.

The title *God's Chaos Code* felt uncomfortable because the Bible says, *"That ye be not soon shaken in mind, or be troubled, neither by spirit, nor by word, nor by letter."*[1] However God and chaos do meet; and out of this meeting, we discover a pattern and design that reveal something profound.

This book, *God's Chaos Code*, was written to help you navigate the convulsions coming to America and the nations. It centers on the Old Testament Hebrew books of Haggai, Ezra, Nehemiah, and Esther. These ancient texts deal with the regathering of Israel after they had been scattered among the nations by Babylon in 605 BC.

The parallels between Israel's regathering and the United States are profound. Why is this period in the Bible so important? The regathering of Israel to their ancient land as a modern nation state in 1948 is one of the greatest fulfillments of prophecy in modern history. As Israel passed its seventieth anniversary in 2018, the Gentile era began to shake. This event further fulfilled the meaning of Jesus's words when he prophesied, *"Jerusalem shall be trodden underfoot of the Gentiles until the time of the Gentiles*

---

1 2 Thessalonians 2:2 (KJV).

is complete."[2] The books about the regathering to Israel under the edict of Cyrus are opening *now*, perhaps because these last books written in the Old Testament are first to be opened.

The prophet Daniel was promised that his writing would be "sealed," only to be "revealed" to God's people at the time of the end.[3] This is, I suggest, the beginning of that time when such Scriptures are revealed.

The Chaos Code reveals a predictive pattern. If I say, "Two, four, six," what comes next? You can make an educated guess and say, "eight." Meaningful patterns are hidden throughout the Bible, from genealogies to sacred feasts. An entire volume could be written on these and other hidden, embedded biblical messages. The Chaos Code covers a sequence that cycles throughout history and targets God's plan for the nations.

The focus of this book is on the patterns and insights impacting America right now and the emerging sheep and goat nations of 2020–2030. A pattern is discovered in the sequence of events, which is what we will be looking at. The prophet Haggai spoke of this time, saying, *"For this is what the LORD of Hosts says: 'Once more, in a little while, I will shake the heavens and the earth, the sea and the dry land. And I will shake all nations, and the desire of all nations shall come: and I will fill this house with glory, says the LORD of hosts.'"*[4] These sequences, patterns, and messages are hidden for us, not from us.

Psalm 2 reveals a conversation. The Father says: *"Ask of me and I will give you the nations for your inheritance, the uttermost parts of the earth for your possession."*[5] It is the Father's intent to glorify the Son—as the King of the nations. This will be imposed without negotiations when He returns. Until then, the King of Glory invites us, as witnesses, to receive the kingdom and to make this kingdom manifest as a witness. How much success should we expect among nations? After His resurrection, Jesus told His disciples to *"Go make disciples of all nations, teaching them …"*[6] He is not waiting for power to do this—*"All power has already been given to Me. Go therefore."*[7] Every country is a prospect.

---

2 Luke 21:24 (KJV).
3 Daniel 12:4 (KJV).
4 Haggai 2:6–7 (NKJV).
5 Psalm 2:8 (KJV).
6 Adapted from Matthew 28:19–20.
7 Adapted from Matthew 28:18.

When the King returns, He will gather all the nations and separate them into the categories of sheep nations and goat nations. Clearly, there will be both sheep and goats at the time of His return. We are alive during the intensification of this process. Some nations, like America, began as a sheep and are being taken over by goats. Others were goats and are becoming sheep. There's a whole lot of shakin' going on, and God Himself is behind much of it. World orders will rise and fall as convulsions of history collapse upon one another, because the kingdom of heaven is putting unbearable pressure on the structures of hell as Jesus draws near. This is the *best* hour to be alive, and *you* need to know that remnants make a difference. Great doors swing on little hinges. The history of the acts of God are tied into the little things that make a big difference.

When you show up, you have the power to alter the trajectory of the storm. Chaotic systems, like hurricanes, are an intimate mix of order and the seemingly random: "From the outside they display unpredictable and chaotic behavior, but expose the inner workings and you discover a perfectly deterministic set of equations ticking like clockwork."[8] What I am describing here is an area of modern mathematics called *Chaos Theory*, a body of research that predicts the behavior of "inherently unpredictable" systems. The origins of Chaos Theory is interesting. With the discovery of the power of computers, a meteorologist began entering in formulas to predict weather patterns like hurricanes. He would enter them at night and come in the day after and discover what the computer came up with, thus finding a way to predict the future path of storms. One night, the computer hit a glitch; and the next day, the meteorologist woke up to discover an entirely different hurricane trajectory heading in another direction! His female assistant found the glitch, and it turned out the hurricane wasn't veering off course—it was the data! A tiny rounding off of a fraction way back in the beginning of the code threw the models off. That seemingly minor detail made a huge difference. God's Chaos Code functions the same way. If God invites you and you don't show up, it impacts what was supposed to happen. When you do show up, God shows up; and that is the fraction that changes everything.

---

8   Jonathan Borwein and Michael Rose, "Explainer; What Is Chaos Theory?" *The Conversation*, Conversation US INC, 18 Nov 2020, https://theconversation.com/explainer-what-is-chaos-theory-10620.

Journey with me through the pages of Scripture as we unlock God's "Chaos Code" and decipher what is next for America and the Nations. The books of revelation are now being opened, and God is speaking to us prophetically from the unsealed books of Haggai, Ezra, Nehemiah, and Esther that cover the events connected to the regathering of Israel. There is a spiritual conflict unfolding now in heavenly places, and the decisive actor in this drama is not Trump, Putin, China, or anyone else—it's you.

CHAPTER 1

THE CODE BEHIND
THE CHAOS

"Verily thou art a God that hidest thyself,
O God of Israel, the Saviour."[1]
—*Isaiah 45:15*

The world is in chaos, and the natural mind cannot see the narrative behind what is really happening. The convulsions seizing our nation are symptomatic of something far more dangerous. But is there a predictable pattern or cycle to America's moments of national crisis? Surprisingly, yes.

While American history never repeats itself in its details, it does rhyme.[2] At the core of our pattern, we discover a new era—called a "turning"—that starts every twenty to twenty-five years. Turnings come in cycles of four, creating a span of four generations (the length of a long life), roughly 80 to 100 years, called a "saeculum." At the start of each turning, the national mood shifts as people adjust how they feel about themselves, the culture, the nation, and what sort of future they expect. When an 80-to-100-year cycle completes, the nation experiences a defining crisis, called a "turning" or "crucible." You and I are alive during America's Fourth Turning—the ultimate crucible.

---

1 Isaiah 45:15 (NKJV)
2 Adapted from "A Quote by Mark Twain." Goodreads. Goodreads. Accessed September 23, 2020. https://www.goodreads.com/quotes/5382-history-doesn-t-repeat-itself-but-it-does-rhyme.

William Strauss and Neil Howe wrote a book describing these cycles, which is especially interesting, since these Ivy league researchers express nowhere any sort of religious beliefs. They are simply studying the cycles of our history.

Consider the turnings that have occurred in the last eighty years:

- **The First Turning:** This is always a *High*. Baby Boomers and those older can recall the great American optimism that followed Victory over Japan Day through the early 1960s and Kennedy's youthful promise.

- **The Second Turning** is a *Consciousness Awakening*. Even Gen-Xers can recall (as kids) the Awareness Revolution, as optimism shifted into a cosmic search, seen in the Jesus Movement as well as the music, free love, and psychedelic drug scene. This began in the '60s and lasted through the early '80s.

- **The Third Turning** is always an *Unraveling*. Every American recalls the most recent third turning because of the era of long economic booms and sudden busts while battle lines in the "culture wars" formed, especially during the mid-'80s as evangelicals learned to organize, communicate, raise funds and get out the vote. This war has continued and collided till today.

- **The Fourth Turning** is always a *Crisis*. It can come early or late in the cycle. The journey from fall to spring requires a winter, which, like the fourth turning, can be severe or mild, but it must come. The only path from "Unraveling" to another "High" is through the stage called "Crisis." Our fourth turning was scheduled to hit somewhere between 2017–2023.

Based on this cycle, America encounters an abrupt *shift* in its collective psyche every twenty years, as a generation enters into a new phase of life. This is true for all turnings in general but is especially amplified in fourth turnings. Each time there is an adjustment to the national mood, it catches everyone by surprise and causes chaos. Consider:

- Colonists did not expect a revolution in 1770.

- Americans, North and South, did not expect a bloody civil war in 1855.

- Once entered, they expected it to be over in six months.

- The roaring twenties did not expect the collapse of the stock market and a Great Depression.[3]

When the fourth turning occurs, it is a crucible that redefines us as a nation. Now in 2020, we are facing another redefining moment. This book, *God's Chaos Code,* offers a way out of the confusion and deceptive media in order to chart a new path forward.

THE OTHER SIDE OF CHAOS

I learned something about chaos while touring through a house turned into a museum in Haarlem, Holland. It is hard to imagine the nearby train station in Amsterdam shipping 400 calm, dignified Jewish people to the horrors of concentration camps every single day. The museum is tucked neatly on the corner of a street lined with shops in the square. The house is preserved to look exactly as it did during the days when German Gestapo boots marched on the cobblestone street outside to arrest the family living inside. They were guilty of the crime of smuggling Jews to safety after hiding them behind an artificial wall in their home. One day, the daughter extended mercy to the wrong person—an informer for the Gestapo. The eighty-year-old father was arrested and died ten days later. The two daughters were sent to Ravensbrück, a notorious women's concentration camp, where one died. The survivor, Corrie ten Boom, wrote *The Hiding Place* to tell her story. At the time of their arrest, they were protecting six Jews—four men and two women—in the cramped, dark hiding place. They were trapped in the small space for forty-two hours, fearing to make a sound because Nazi guards remained in the house after the family was arrested. After forty-two hours, the Nazi guards were replaced by local police. The local police knew about the ten Boom underground and supported their mission. Once they discovered the Jews

---

3   William Strauss and Neil Howe, *The Fourth Turning: An American Prophecy,* (New York: Bantam Doubleday Dell, 1997), 2–6.

in the hiding place they were able to smuggle them to safety. The ten Booms were Christians who believed they were called to love all people, regardless of their faith.

Years later, Corrie ten Boom traveled the world and spoke about her experience. She carried with her a piece of tapestry to illustrate that God rules over darkness and works out his sovereign purposes in all things. On the back of the tapestry, the pattern was chaotic and without a discernible form. Corrie ten Boom would say that this is like life; sometimes it does not make sense. Then she would flip the cloth over and reveal a beautiful pattern of a crown on the other side. She would recite the poem: *Life is But a Weaving.*

> Not till the loom is silent and the shuttles cease to fly
> Will God unroll the canvas and reveal the reason why.
> The dark threads are as needful in the weaver's skillful hand
> As the threads of gold and silver in the pattern He has planned.
> He knows, He loves, He cares; nothing this truth can dim.
> He gives the very best to those who leave the choice to Him.[4]

God is in the midst of the unraveling, and He is working out His plan. We just need to see the grand design through heaven's eyes. Your life is a thread, tied into the complex and majestic grand design of the story that began in Genesis. God's *Logos,* the Word of God, hovered over the chaos of a formless void. The word for this void in Hebrew is the word *Tohu va-Vohu,* which describes a condition of confusion and unfathomable chaos. God hovers over this condition and brings out something beautiful. Looking at the earth, we see the void; but looking through heaven's eyes, we see the design. The Word of God, the Logos, gives us eyes to see what is happening.

People long for prophetic perspective during a period of intense crisis. This happened after 9/11 as preachers flooded the marketplace with books; some were good, but many were wildly inaccurate. The prophetic aspect of the Bible is, however, the secret to peace of mind.

---

4 Corrie ten Boom, "Life is but a Weaving (The Tapestry Poem)," WordPress, February 21, 2018. https://thepoetryplace.wordpress.com/2018/02/21/ life-is-but-a-weaving-the-tapestry-poem-by-corrie-ten-boom/

There is a sequence to prophetic events that unfold in the midst of chaos. The apostle Paul warned his churches to *"be not soon shaken in mind, or be troubled, neither by spirit, nor by word, nor by letter as from us, as that the day of Christ is at hand."*[5] Understanding what the Bible actually teaches about our day will help you *"not be shaken in mind, or troubled."*[6] Rather than a spirit of fear, you will have a sound mind in the midst of shaking. Your focus will be on what God is saying and not on trendy conspiracy theories.

The key to understanding our crisis is to step back and see the picture of what God is doing in the nations. Like Corrie ten Boom's embroidery, on the other side of all the chaos is God's beautiful tapestry. Understanding how to look at life through heaven's eye is what *God's Chaos Code* is all about.

Unlocking the code is important because we are being plunged into a period of time foreseen by prophets but veiled to previous generations. The Chaos Code reveals a pattern of events woven into Jewish history that parallels what is taking place today. The books of Haggai, Zechariah, Ezra, Nehemiah, and Esther are a chronology of events that are key to understanding why America and the nations of the earth are experiencing chaos.

The code is deciphered when we break down the sequence of events surrounding the regathering of Israel in 538 BC. In Jewish history there were two periods of divine judgement when the inhabitants of Jerusalem were driven out of the land under shackles of slavery as their city was reduced to rubble. This shocking dislocation took place under the hands of Babylon in 605 BC and again by Rome in AD 70. Each time this happened, it was followed by a miraculous regathering and rebuilding. It is the first regathering, out of Babylon under the decree of Cyrus, that is covered in the books being opened to us. This is the source of our code. The second miraculous regathering of Israel to their land occurred in 1948. We are alive in the period of the final regathering of Israel. The sequence of events unfolding in our day run on a remarkable parallel track to the story of their first regathering under Cyrus. So much so that the books could have been written for our generation. The subject literally jumps off the pages as it is opened to us now by the Spirit of God, in a new and

---

5 2 Thessalonians 2:2 (Darby Bible).

6 Adapted from 2 Thessalonians 2:2

powerful way. What was irrelevant to us ten years ago now speaks with startling clarity and power. The types, patterns, and sequence of events are so clear that anyone can understand the Chaos Code.

Imagine a safe-cracker with his ear to the vault as he turns the tumblers left and then right and then left, and hears a "click." You'll hear the "click" the moment you realize that today's events are part of a predictive pattern that has already occurred. That's the code. Now, imagine this delicate process taking place with all sorts of noise, explosions, and disinformation going on at the same time—that's the chaos.

THE CODE BEGINS WITH CYRUS

The code has five parts to it: Each letter in the word *CHAOS* represents a stage in the sequence of what is happening in nations right now. Different nations are in different stages of the code. While the Chaos Code is revealed in the regathering of Israel back to Jerusalem in 538 BC, the sequence is repeating itself today. The first "click" in the Chaos Code is "C" which stands for "Cyrus-type" rulers. These Cyrus rulers emerge in nations when a cry goes up from God's people to restore traditional and religious values.

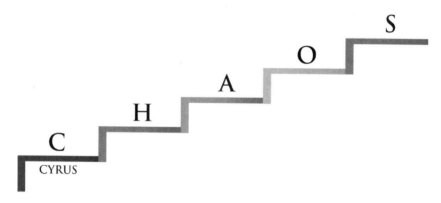

God's Chaos Code—5 steps out of chaos and into an unshakable kingdom

These Cyrus types resist the deteriorating influences on culture, families, and national identity. They are often plain-spoken, non-religious types. They lead their nations in a path that resists the destructive influences that are destroying culture in the West, and they fight for the independence of their national sovereignty in the face of pressure to collapse their boundaries to unwise immigration or the economic global order. Cyrus-type rulers emerge in response to the prevailing prayers of God's people.

At this point we should look at the overlapping roles of each individual God used to shape the era of Israel's regathering. The main actors are Isaiah, Jeremiah, Cyrus, and Daniel. It was Daniel who emerged as an indispensable intercessor whom God used to unlock the Chaos Code of his day. A word should be said about the role of prophets in Israel's history. They were indispensable to the sanity of the Hebrews because they predicted in astonishing detail the events that would happen to their people. For instance, Isaiah was a prophet in 740 BC who predicted the destruction and restoration of Jerusalem 120 years before Babylon was even on the map! The next great prophet in the sequence of the code is Jeremiah in 627 BC. It is likely that Daniel heard the prophet Jeremiah speak before his departure to Babylon in the first wave of deported Jews.

To Daniel, Jeremiah stood out as the one prophet to accurately predict the fall of Jerusalem, and therefore, Daniel studied Jeremiah's prophecies even while living in Babylon. Jeremiah's letters promised the exiles that God had good plans for His people and that they should settle down for the seventy-year exile and seek the peace of the city, *"for in their peace you shall have peace"*[7]—wise advice for the church that lives in Babylonian territory. Daniel studied further, looking for a key to the timing of their release. He sensed a change was at hand for his people. He studied the letters written by Jeremiah to those in exile.

As Daniel read, he saw it! *"For thus says the Lord, after seventy years are completed at Babylon, I will visit you and perform My good word toward you and cause you to return to this place."*[8]

Daniel knew with certainty that the Babylonian captivity would not last forever. He did some quick math and realized he was in a seventy-year divine window of time, and the transition from Babylon to Persia was at hand.

The end of the Babylonian rule would take place in one day. The transition began with a feast. Nebuchadnezzar's grandson, Belteshazzar, gathered a thousand rulers together for an opulent banquet full of debaucherous revelry and feasting. As the party atmosphere reached a peak, Belteshazzar called for

---

7 Jeremiah 29:7 (WEB).
8 Jeremiah 29:10 (NKJV).

the sacred gold vessels, seized from the Hebrew temple seventy years earlier by his grandfather. One by one, they lifted the vessels, laughed, and made toasts to their demon idols of gold and silver. They threw the party with full knowledge of the military expedition against them already underway by Cyrus, the king of Persia, but felt secure in their impregnable stronghold. The city walls were eighty-seven feet wide and could host chariot races. There was no way through the walls, as the River Euphrates provided a protective moat, covering all four sides of the city. An attacking army either had to build a bulwark that would go over the wall or tunnel under the wall, which was impossible in Babylon's case because of the large moat of the Euphrates.

Suddenly the revelry stopped. The people gasped in horror at the appearance of a disembodied hand writing on the wall in a mysterious language. King Belteshazzar was stricken with terror. Little did they know that the gold vessels from the Jewish temple that they were drinking from represented the tragic tale of the servants of God taken hostage to Babylon. Daniel, the man they summoned to decipher the message, was one of them.

The message inscribed on the wall said:

"MENE MENE TEKEL UPHARSIN"[9]

Daniel studied the language, deciphered the code, and delivered the verdict that would end the era of Babylonian rule: *"You have been weighed in the balances, and found wanting."*[10] As Daniel was delivering the message, Cyrus and his armies were entering the impregnable city by way of an engineering feat that diverted a portion of the Euphrates upstream. By this means, the army of Cyrus could enter the city by crouching under the gates. The conquest of Babylon was as swift as it was unexpected, and virtually bloodless. Half the metropolis was under Persian rule before the rest were aware, least of all Belteshazzar. The party dispersed; and as for Belteshazzar, *"In that night was Belshazzar the king of the Chaldeans slain."*[11] Nations and empires, we will find, have defined boundaries and time periods. When the time is up, a new chapter of history opens.[12]

---

9 Daniel 5:25 (NKJV).
10 Daniel 5:27 (NKJV).
11 Daniel 5:30 (KJV).
12 See Acts 17:26.

The Persian king Cyrus took Babylon in 538 BC. Supernatural assistance was given to him in his conquest. The angel Gabriel told Daniel, *"I, even I, stood up to confirm and strengthen him."*[13] It is a matter of great interest that there was angelic warfare taking place to make sure the right heathen ruler was seated on this throne. The defining issue for selecting a political candidate should not be, "Are they a Christian?" A Lincoln or Churchill or Cyrus could be missed, and a counterfeit, who knows how to play to the religious, could be put in office. Cyrus rulers are not typically religious.

GOD'S LOVE LETTER TO CYRUS

With Cyrus in place, the next great event on God's timeline was the fulfillment of Jeremiah's prophecy: the release of the exiles from their seventy years of captivity. The historian, Josephus, explains how Cyrus arrived at this decision. In the first year of Cyrus's reign, Daniel showed Cyrus the writings of Isaiah, addressing Cyrus by name. Written 120 years earlier, the prophecy is remarkable in its details, right down to Cyrus's entering Babylon by drying up and crossing the Euphrates river. Isaiah even added a description of the famed "double doors" at the entrance of Babylon. The majestic entrance to the city was a massive double gate, flanked with bright towers of blue enameled brick. The prophecy was even more remarkable in light of the fact that at the time of Isaiah, Babylon did not have these doors and was not yet a world power. Neither did the majestic temple of Solomon and the city of Jerusalem need to be rebuilt. Put yourself in the seat of Cyrus, and imagine reading a letter from God written to you by name 120 years before you were born.

> *I am the Lord,*
> *the Maker of all things...*
> *Who says to the deep, "Be dry!*
> *And I will **dry up your rivers**";*
> ***Who says of Cyrus**, "He is My shepherd,*
> *And he shall perform all My pleasure",*
> *Saying to Jerusalem, "You shall **be built**,"*
> *And to **the temple**, "Your foundation shall be laid."*
> *Thus says the Lord to His anointed,*

---

13 Daniel 11:1 (NKJV).

To Cyrus, *whose right hand I have held—*
To subdue nations *before him*
And loose the armor of kings,
To **open before him the double doors,**
So that the gates will not be shut:
I will go before you
and will level the mountains;
so that you may know that I am the Lord,
the God of Israel, **who summons you by name.**
That you may know that **I, the Lord,**
Who call you by your name,
Am the God of Israel.[14]

When Cyrus read this, the Spirit of the Lord came upon him. The Bible recounts in the book of Ezra, "*Now in the first year of Cyrus king of Persia, that the word of the Lord by the mouth of the prophet Jeremiah might be fulfilled,* **the LORD stirred up the spirit of Cyrus** *King of Persia, so that he made a proclamation throughout all his kingdom, and also put it in writing …*"[15]

Ezra's writing tells us that the decree of Cyrus sent off a shock wave in the Jewish community in Babylon. Immediately, 49,897 Jews volunteered to make the arduous journey to Jerusalem as the first wave of refugees returning home. This decree marked the beginning of the prophetic moment the Jewish people were waiting for. As we will see in the story of Israel's regathering, in the midst of earthly chaos God's unseen tapestry of spiritual activity was weaving together prophets, intercessors, and political developments to impact nations and advance His agenda on the earth.

NATIONS ENTER THE VALLEY OF DECISION

It is impossible to separate Israel from God's Chaos Code, as the Lord has promised to return to Jerusalem and to reign from Jerusalem. Jesus prophesied that the rulers would reject Him and that the Jewish nation would be scattered. He also foresaw the return of His people and that they would

---

14 Isaiah 44:24, 27—45:3 (NKJV).
15 Ezra 1:1–4 (NKJV).

have partial and then complete control of Jerusalem saying, *"Jerusalem will be trampled underfoot by the Gentiles, until the times of the Gentiles are fulfilled."*[16]

The Jewish nation's second dispersion from their land was at the hands of the Romans in AD 70. It would take nearly 1,878 years for something to happen that has never happened to another nation. After being driven out of their homeland and dispersed over the earth, the Jewish people returned and were recognized as a *nation in 1948*. Prime Minister David Ben-Gurion proclaimed on May 14, 1948, the establishment of the State of Israel. The US president at the time was Harry S. Truman; he threw his weight behind the recognition of the new nation that same day. Asked if he knew about the role of Cyrus in the Bible, Truman, a man of Trumpian temperament, knew this part of the Bible and said, "I am Cyrus."

This second regathering would correspond to two significant dates in the future of Israel: the regathering of Israel back into their homeland and the times of the Gentiles being fulfilled as Israel retook the city of Jerusalem in 1967. To understand the grand architecture of events, you have to recognize that Israel is the missing piece. Now that Israel has been regathered, Jerusalem enters the picture. Through His prophetic Word, God has declared to all nations that He intends to regather Israel in their own land and restore them to His favor. He has also made it clear that He will intervene in judgment against those nations who oppress Israel or resist God's purposes for them.

The issues that thus confront all nations are set forth clearly in Joel: *"In those days and at that time when I restore the fortunes of Judah and Jerusalem I will gather all nations and bring them down to the Valley of Jehoshaphat."*[17]

Once in this valley, all nations will be forced to make a decision. In 2017, with a stroke of a pen, we entered the first stage of this development.

"MR. PRESIDENT, YOU ARE CYRUS"

After Donald Trump's election, anti-Trump pundits were agitated and perplexed by the overwhelming support from the faith community. Trump's stunning victory became the immediate obsession of news

---

16 Luke 21:24 (NASB).
17 Joel 3:1–2 (NIV).

analysts. He won by razor-thin margins in five swing states, and the questions from pundits narrowed down to, "What happened? Who exactly was it that voted for him?" It was a last-minute turnout of Christians who felt America was heading over a cliff. Writers and researchers dashed off into Red State America to ask, "How can you be a Christian and justify your support for Trump?" The answer that kept coming back was that, "Donald Trump is a modern-day Cyrus."

That was how my name came up in the media. As soon as the data started coming out about the Cyrus narrative, my phone started blowing up with alerts. My prediction that "Donald Trump was God's Cyrus" evidently took hold. The comments kept coming in from *Mother Jones, The Daily Beast, Vox, Salon, The New York Times*—and they were all hostile.

HBO's *Politically Incorrect with Bill Maher* was my favorite put-down. Maher was running a video with me leading off a montage of other preachers, increasingly eccentric, preaching about Cyrus Trump. In mocking exasperation, he cut to the camera and said, "Who the [bleep] is Cyrus?" He was genuinely befuddled.

Then suddenly it all stopped. In a moment, as unexpected as it was explosive, Donald Trump made the historic decision to move the US embassy from Tel Aviv to Jerusalem.

On December 6, 2017, the United States recognized Jerusalem as the undivided capital of Israel. Trump was warned that doing so would risk igniting a religious war across the already-turbulent Middle East. Trump's decision was categorically rejected by a majority of world leaders. Surprisingly, Britain, France, Sweden, Italy, and Japan were among the critical countries. As it turned out, they were wrong and he was right. There was no war following his decision. The word I received in 2015—"The 45th president of the United states will be an Isaiah 45 ruler, and he will be likened to King Cyrus"—was fulfilled by Donald Trump making a decree regarding the establishment of Israel as a nation, just like Cyrus did 2,500 years ago. This move happened on May 14, 2018, seventy years to the day that Prime Minister David Ben-Gurion proclaimed the establishment of the State of Israel.

The United Nations General Assembly immediately held an emergency session on December 7, 2017. During the security council's meeting, fourteen out of fifteen members condemned Trump's decision. Subsequently, on December 21, 2017, the UN voted, and 128 nations rejected the embassy move while nine nations stood in favor (Guatemala, Hondu-ras, Israel, Marshall Islands, Federated States of Micronesia, Nauru, Palau, Togo, and the United States) and thirty-five nations were *absent.*

So what does this UN vote mean? It means that friendship with Israel is a moral decision that has a very small upside but a huge downside. The Jews have been linked to Jerusalem since David took the city and made it his capital in 1010 BC. Who would deny their right to a homeland with Jeru-salem as their capital? There are only 14.6 million[18] people self-identifying as Jews. Islamic nations are much larger. There are 1.8 billion[19] Muslims. Obviously, Muslims are a bigger market and, in many places, openly hos-tile to Israel. The nations that voted for Israel are predominantly Christian. While the world watched, it wasn't just the UN taking a vote that day; I believe heaven was also keeping score. It will happen a few more times as nations are brought into the valley of decision and are forced to decide if they will do what is right regarding Israel or do what benefits themselves.

After the embassy move, I was still being harangued about calling Trump a modern-day Cyrus. All of that stopped suddenly on March 5, 2018, when Israel's Prime Minister Benjamin Netanyahu was at the White House to recognize the president's embassy decision. He said:

"Mr. President, I want to tell you that the Jewish people have a long memory, so we remember the proclamation of the great king, Cyrus the great, a Persian king twenty-five hundred years ago. He proclaimed that the Jewish exiles in Babylon could come back and rebuild our temple in Jerusalem ... We remember how a few weeks ago, President Donald J. Trump recognized Jerusalem as Israel's capital."[20] Netanyahu continued, "Mr. President, this will be remembered by our people through the ages." To the consternation

18 "Jewish Population by Country." Wikipedia. Wikimedia Foundation, September 23, 2020. https://en.wikipedia.org/wiki/Jewish_population_by_country.

19 "Muslim World." Wikipedia. Wikimedia Foundation, September 15, 2020. https://en.wikipedia.org/wiki/Muslim_world.

20 Andrew Silow-Carroll. "Who Is King Cyrus, and Why Did Netanyahu Compare Him to Trump?" *The Times of Israel.* The Times of Israel, March 8, 2018. https://www.timesofisrael.com/who-is-king-cyrus-and-why-is-netanyahu-comparing-him-to-trump/.

of all the comedians and reporters who had been mocking me, Netanyahu officially linked Trump to the Old Testament King Cyrus.

Rabbis in Israel [21] commemorated the historic move—and put the final nail in the coffin of the news media's hysteria—when they minted a Trump/Cyrus coin in celebration of the US Embassy move. Donald Trump's profile is superimposed over King Cyrus's on one side, and the third temple is pictured on the other. It's called the "temple coin." During the primaries leading up to the 2016 election, I made this Cyrus prediction and nine others about Donald Trump and the future of America. Seven have been fulfilled, and three are unfolding now. To see them all, visit: *lancewallnau.com/predictions*.

To the media's further dismay, a year later, Trump recognized Israel's sovereignty over the Golan Heights;[22] and they were again dismayed when Netanyahu linked Trump to Cyrus. "In the long sweep of Jewish history," declared the prime minister, "there have been a handful of proclamations by non-Jewish leaders on behalf of our people and our land: Cyrus the Great, the great Persian king; Lord Balfour; president Harry S. Truman; and President Donald J. Trump."[23]

At this point, a blind man could not miss it—Donald Trump is a Cyrus leader. This, however, does not mean that all Christians accept this fact. A surprising number of the evangelical Sanhedrin are either slow or unwilling to recognize something historic when it takes place in front of their eyes.

---

21 Molly Hunter. "Israeli Group Sells Special-Edition Trump Coin." ABC News. ABC News Network, May 11, 2018. https://abcnews.go.com/International/israeli-group-sells-special-edition-trump-coin/story?id=55096698.

22 Mark and David Landler. "Trump, With Netanyahu, Formally Recognizes Israel's Authority Over Golan Heights." The New York Times. The New York Times, March 25, 2019. https://www.nytimes.com/2019/03/25/us/politics/benjamin-netanyahu-donald-trump-meeting.html.

23 Tuly Weisz. "Unto the Nations: Trump Isn't Cyrus—Yet." The Jerusalem Post | JPost.com. The Jerusalem Post, March 27, 2019. https://www.jpost.com/opinion/unto-the-nations-trump-isnt-cyrus-yet-584939.

CYRUS SIGHTINGS AROUND THE GLOBE

In 2016, I believed the only person that fit this description of an Isaiah 45 Cyrus ruler was Donald Trump, but I was wrong. In the last three-and-a-half years, I've identified other Cyrus-type leaders all over the globe. At the time of this writing, they can be seen in America, the UK, Poland, the Republic of Georgia, Hungary, Australia, Brazil, Guatemala, and Israel. God has raised up these secular leaders to preserve national borders, customs, culture, language, and religious heritage.

- **President Andrzej Duda**, of Poland officially recognized Jesus Christ as King of Poland in Krakow, on November 19, 2016. He called upon Jesus to rule over the nation, its people, and its political leaders. The people are seeking to rediscover their Christian roots after years of lost history to Nazis and atheist Soviet domination. Poland's constitution is one of seven in the European Union to ban same-sex marriage. In 2017, thousands of Polish Catholics formed a human chain on the nation's border, interceding for God to spare Poland, Europe, and the world from aggressive Islamization. They welcome all people, races, and ethnicities but will not compromise their quest for Christian civilization.

- **Prime Minister Viktor Orbán**, of Hungary. He is a Trumpian figure who said in 2011, "We believe that our children and grandchildren will make Hungary great again," and his conservative moral and religious policies have produced political and economic stability while reversing a declining birth rate. Orbán built a barbed-wire fence (a wall) along Hungary's border with Serbia to stop migrants and refugees from entering the country and is cracking down on "fake news."[24] In 2018, Orbán correctly assessed George Soros's destabilizing influence and took action to cut it off. "We are fighting an enemy that is different from us. Not open, but hiding; not straightforward but crafty; not honest but base; not national but international; does not believe in working but speculates with

---

24 See Kovacs, Zoltan. "The Politics And Meddling Of Soros And The Open Society Network. " *About Hungary,* IMPRESSUM, 31 Jan 2018. http://abouthungary. hu/blog/the-politics-and-meddling-of-soros-and-the-open-society-network/

money; does not have its own homeland but feels it owns the whole world,"[25] Orbán states, "If we look at our Europe in terms of the spirit of religion we see that it has rejected it's Christian foundations."[26]

- **President Jair Bolsonaro**, of Brazil, is nicknamed "the Trump of the tropics." A February 6, 2020, *Fox News* article states, "As he heads into his second year as Brazil's first right–wing president in four elections, Jair Bolsonaro is remaining steadfast in his Trumpian, culture warrior style of leadership." The article goes on to say, "The former army captain rose to power on a platform of confronting what he saw as a swelling socialist ideology, rooting out rampant corruption, cracking down on crime and reviving Brazil's sluggish economy … Bolsonaro has made his evangelicalism central to his leadership. In a national address just before Christmas 2019, Bolsonaro said he 'took over Brazil in a deep ethical, moral and economic crisis.' … The government has changed. Today we have a president who cherishes families, respects the will of its people, honors its military and believes in God,' the Brazilian president said."[27]

In this hour, Cyrus rulers are rising to preserve their nations' religious values from the Western virus of cultural decay. They will not sacrifice the unique identity of their nation to an emerging global system, especially one hostile to Christians and Jews. These leaders may not seem religious, but they will govern in a manner that guards what is sacred for their nations at large. Trump, like these other Cyrus leaders, is a populist.

This is nothing less than a global populist movement rising like a wave and pushing back on the forces trying to tear down family, religious

---

25 Zack Beauchamp. "Hungary Just Passed a 'Stop Soros' Law That Makes It Illegal to Help Undocumented Migrants." *Vox.* Vox, June 22, 2018. https://www.vox.com/policy-and-politics/2018/6/22/17493070/hungary-stop-soros-orban.

26 Tusnádfürdő. "Prime Minister Viktor Orbán's Speech at the 29th Bálványos Summer Open University and Student Camp." About Hungary. IMPRESSUM, July 30, 2018. http://abouthungary.hu/speeches-and-remarks/prime-minister-viktor-orbans-speech-at-the-29th-balvanyos-summer-open-university-and-student-camp/.

27 Morgan Phillips. "Jair Bolsonaro: What to Know about Brazil's Controversial President." Fox News. FOX News Network, February 6, 2020. https://www.foxnews.com/world/who-is-jair-bolsonaro-brazil.

foundations, territorial integrity, and love of nation. This wave is putting a new political force into office representing a conservative backlash against the trends that have eroded culture and collapsed boundaries. These Cyrus rulers share fundamental core beliefs:

- The preservation of modern nation states against socialism

- The preservation of borders against collectivism

- The preservation of the family and faith, and the belief that God, not government, is the foundation of civilization

The point is that Cyrus seems to be a type of secular ruler being raised up for the sake of God's people. And when they show up there is a sequence of events kicked off. They usher in a window of grace for God's people to come out from under oppression and do the work of rebuilding their nation. In the next four chapters, we are going to look at the rest of the Chaos Code to prophetically predict what is coming after Cyrus.

ISRAEL'S ANCIENT FUTURIST'S

As Israel's nomadic journey unfolded, there was a tribe of scholars called the tribe of Issachar that provided direction in times of confusion. They had a gift for "*understanding the times and knowing what Israel ought to do* ."[28]

Issachar was the fifth son of the patriarch Jacob, whose twelve sons make up the twelve tribes of Israel. Though small in number, this tribe held a unique role of command among their brethren.[29] The tribe of Levi, a tribe of teaching priests, consulted with Issachar at critical junctures in history in order to clarify what Israel ought to do in the midst of their own tumultuous transitions.

Issachar's gift was to accurately forecast the future in light of what was unfolding by:

- **Reviewing** Israel's *past* to discern patterns for the future

- **Evaluating** *present* day events

- **Investigating** *prophetic* words that are possibly unfolding

---

28 Adapted from 1 Chronicles 12:32.
29 Adapted from 1 Chronicles 12:32.

From those three sources—past, present, and prophetic—the tribe of Issachar could, by the Spirit of God, intuit what was about to come next. They were *scriptural futurists*—and very accurate.

When the scripture says Issachar "understood the times" we should ask, what were the times the writer was talking about? Surprisingly, the issue of their day was both political and spiritual. They were being consulted about who was called to rule the nation. The future was with a young shepherd boy who slayed the Philistine giant named Goliath. David was anointed by God to be the next king of Israel. The only problem was that the current king, Saul, was in power and hunting his successor. Because Issachar understood the times, they knew a transition of spiritual government was taking place and the time had come to cast their support behind David. This choice was important because other tribes were prepared to do the same, once Issachar was on board. They, like us today, were caught in a time between the times.

We live at a time when the future is invading the present. The powers of the age to come are pressing into the age that is. The time of harvest is the time when all things ripen to full maturity. Darkness covers the earth, but the glory of the Lord shines out in greater contrast. Evil men, we are told, "*wax worse and worse,*"[30] and yet the overcoming Church is made even more resplendent as the "*bride hath made herself ready.*"[31] As the "*times of the Gentiles*"[32] close, we will be inexorably drawn back to the drama of Israel, that sliver of earth no larger than New Jersey. History must cycle back to the land where the Messiah declared He will return. The shaking of nations will accelerate, not because of the devil, but because the Lord is on the move. One of the great prophets of the code era is Ezekiel. He saw this time and prophesied: "*I will overturn, overturn, overturn, it: and it shall be no more, until he come whose right it is; and I will give it Him.*"[33]

Like the tribe of Issachar, in this book we are going to take today's headlines, overlay them with the code found in the story of Israel's regathering, and see what was, what is, and what is coming next. The actors in our generation can change and the Cyrus-type leaders can rotate, but the cycle that makes up the Chaos Code is timeless and continues to unfold with uncanny accuracy.

---

30 2 Kings 3:13 (KJV)
31 Adapted from Revelation 19:7
32 Luke 21:24 (KJV)
33 Ezekiel 21:27 (KJV)

CHAPTER 2

A HOUSE FOR THE NATION

"Sometimes while you are so passionately busy building, there will be others as busy destroying. Do not stop. One day you will notice how high above you get, and how down below they end up."[1]
—*Sameh Elsayed*

Both the Old and New Testaments predict that everything that can be shaken *will* be shaken. What is shaking now is the political and social order of America and nations worldwide. According to the Bible, this shaking is inevitable. Why? Because there is a cosmic battle for nations. The shaking is happening because there is a spiritual architecture, an invisible hierarchy of powers, that militates against God and His plan for the nations.

The apostle Paul describes the Christian struggle as a contest against, *"principalities and powers and rulers of the darkness of this world."*[2] As hard as it is to comprehend, the origin of the chaos isn't physical; it's spiritual. The cosmic shaking forecast for this era engages both heaven and earth, the unseen and the seen. Visible earthly thrones are a reflection of thrones that are invisible. God has made it clear that the hosts of heaven, the angelic

---

1 "A Quote By Sameh Elsayed." Goodreads. Goodreads Inc, 2020, https://www. goodreads.com/quotes/3208849-sometimes-while-you-are-so-passionately-busy-building-there-will.
2 Adapted from Ephesians 6:12.

armies, are systematically and progressively laying siege to resisting powers in the heavens, the realm of *"spiritual wickedness in heavenly places."*[3] God is building something in the midst of the rise and fall of powers in the present world order. Each convulsion and shaking is working toward a final outcome: the emergence of God's unshakable kingdom on the earth.

The shakings are a signal; God has given us four warnings to tell us that America is being weighed in the balance. In February of 2020, America had accumulated $5 trillion dollars in increased wealth and was experiencing a record low 3.6 percent unemployment rate, the lowest in forty-nine years. Those record economic gains and jobless numbers were something Obama never thought was possible. Who can forget his saying in the 2016 town hall, "Some jobs of the past are just never going to come back." Obama sarcastically went on to ask how Trump was going to get those jobs back. "What magic wand do you have?"[4] Obama, like many others, underestimated Trump's fierce negotiating skills that would get Americans back to work and lock in and renegotiate trade deals.

In fact, in April of 2019, there were more jobs available than people seeking employment! When the COVID-19 pandemic happened, businesses across the country were closed, people were mandated to stay at home, and the American economy shook in ways we haven't seen since the 1930's Great Depression. As a result, by July 2020, 51 million Americans had filed for unemployment benefits. In three months, America lost all the economic gains we had achieved during Trump's presidency. Thank God, we had had the growth we did, or America would be in far worse shape than we are today. To the spiritually discerning mind, this was the *first warning* to America that the nation was undergoing an assault against its very economic survival.

The *second warning* alarm went off as debt multiplied. To protect American jobs and keep companies in business, the president and the 116th US Congress passed a relief package that brought our national debt to a dangerously high $26 trillion. Trump inherited $20 trillion of national debt on his inauguration day and warned before running for office that $22 trillion

---

3 Ephesians 6:12 (King James 2000 Bible)

4 *BlazeTV.* "Trump Makes Obama Regret His Jobs Prediction." May 3, 2019. Video, 1:14. https://www.youtube.com/watch?v=AqzoO-Hu1mk

in debt was a dangerous tipping point to watch. Once the national debt exceeds the GDP, the nation's economic survival is at risk.

When you combine the *first and second warnings,* you see how the economic shaking of America has been accelerated by the release of the China virus. Seen from the perspective of spiritual thrones, the emerging dominant world influence of the Chinese Communist Party (CCP) is laying siege to the world order. Its intended impact is to take down its greatest spiritual rival, the United States. It is important to note that there is a difference between the party and the Chinese people. For years, there has been a close and sympathetic rapport with the Church in China, whose numbers are estimated at 100 million. Rather, this is a contest between the Chinese Communist Party dragon wrestling with the eagle. The eagle can win, because when the battle is fought in economic terms, the total aggregate economic power of a nation is measured in terms of GDP. The US GDP under Trump is $20 trillion dollars, and the China GDP is only $11 trillion. However, the eagle is no match for a full-grown dragon. The impact the virus has had on the global economy is unprecedented, and it will redefine all nations as they grapple with its aftermath, particularly China and the United States.

The *third unmistakable warning* was the tragic circumstances surrounding the death of George Floyd. Met with a universal outcry, Americans nationwide took to the streets to protest. After seeing the video footage of George's death, as a nation we were united in outrage against the needless use of force. Philonise Floyd, George Floyd's brother, appeared before a House Judiciary Committee and said:

> People of all backgrounds, genders and race have come together to demand change. Honor them, honor George, and make the necessary changes that make law enforcement the solution—and not the problem. Hold them accountable when they do something wrong. Teach them what it means to treat people with empathy and respect. Teach them what necessary force is. Teach them that deadly force should be used rarely and only when life is at risk.[5]

---

5 William Cummings "'Look what you did, big brother. You're changing the world.' Read Philonise Floyd's opening statement." USA Today. https://www.usatoday.com/story/news/politics/2020/06/10/george-floyd-read-philonise-floyds-opening-statement-congress/5333335002/

We all shared an ardent desire to see better training for police officers and more accountability; yet when protests morphed into rioting and violence in the name of George Floyd, we began to see something ominous in the wind.

The riots escalated to an all-out assault—tearing down historic statues, spray-painting graffiti on federal monuments, destroying small businesses, burning police precincts, flags, Bibles—and even churches. Verbal intimidation expanded into violent assaults on city streets. We watched in shock as *everyday* Americans were accosted and United States Senators harangued. Then we were horrified to discover that two unarmed Trump supporters had been assassinated in cold blood.

This wasn't a peaceful protest; this was a Marxist *revolution*. This "revolution" was a *fourth warning*. Antifa and BLM became the well-funded and organized tip of the spear in a series of public assaults. They were, and still are, supported by Silicon Valley and corporations while operating under the cover of Democrat-aligned media and politicians. Antifa is a revolutionary global militia movement, organized in multiple cells. In America, they aspire to forcibly overthrow the United States government. According to journalist Andy Ngo, whose parents escaped communist Vietnam in the 1970s, Antifa operates as a paramilitary structure. He observes, "Scouts monitor the perimeter of an area and provide live audio and text updates. There are street medics, trained to get injured comrades out. And there are those who carry out violence with weapons and firebombs. They use encrypted smartphone apps to signal and communicate."[6]

As the US economy claws its way back and unemployment recovers, under all this America is still shaking. The daily specter of Marxist militia, flash protests, and anarchy is leaving many people desperate to know, *How will all this end?* The answer to what happens next is found in the Chaos Code, in the books of Haggai and Zechariah.

THE HIDDEN PATTERN CONTINUES

In the code, Cyrus showed up as a *sign* to God's people that the regathering of Israel was about to take place. Certain prophetic events create a *boundary marker* or item in the timeline of history. A boundary item marks the end of

---

6 Adapted from Andy Ngô. "Antifa Are Organized in Multiple Units." Thread Reader. June 1, 2020. https://threadreaderapp.com/thread/1267479754136928256.html.

something and a new beginning. You and I create boundary items in our own lives to mark transitions, such as birthdays, weddings, or funerals. Many of the stories in the Bible do the same thing. For example, the star that showed up at the time of Christ's birth was a sign, marking the beginning of a new era.

In the new era of Israel's regathering, the emergence of Cyrus was a boundary item, marking the end of Babylonian captivity. Cyrus marked the fulfillment of a prophecy spoken by Jeremiah that the Jewish people would be released from Babylon after seventy years of servitude. It marked the end of God's judgment and the beginning of a new assignment—to rebuild Jerusalem.

This building project was the next step in God's prophetic timeline after Cyrus was put in office. As we will see, their obedience will unleash God's blessings from heaven and their disobedience will release economic judgment. Wrapped in this Bible story is what we as the Church are facing today. Have we, as the global Church, lost sight of our God-given assignment, and could the economic shaking and subsequent calamities be a wake-up call that all is not right in the house of God?

THEIR STORY IS OUR STORY

To lead the Jews back to Jerusalem and fulfill the mandate to rebuild the temple, Cyrus authorized Zerubbabel, the head of the tribe of Judah, to organize the return of the Jewish people, appointing him as governor. The Spirit that stirred Cyrus to make the decree now stirred 49,000 people to respond and make the four-month, 900-mile journey to Jerusalem.[7]

"Then rose up the heads of the fathers' houses of Judah and Benjamin, and the priests and the Levites, everyone whose spirit God had stirred to go up to rebuild the house of the LORD that is in Jerusalem."[8]

After arriving in Jerusalem, Zerubbabel set out immediately to rebuild the temple; and in the second month of the second year of the return, the foundation was laid. They threw a huge party with all the modest fanfare that could be commanded. They were rebuilding on the site of Solomon's temple, the first temple. Their achievement was a profound contrast with

---

7 "Ezra Fact #7: How Long Was the Journey from Babylon to JeruSalem?" ESV Bible. Crossway. Accessed September 23, 2020. https://www.esv.org/resources/esv-global-study-bible/facts-ezra-7/.
8 Ezra 1:5 (ESV).

the grandeur of Solomon's enterprise. Almost immediately, the building project began to slow and eventually stop because the Samaritans, who inhabited the land, resisted them. This would continue for sixteen years.

What happened? The Bible says their enemies hired "counselors" against them. Counselors were legal and political consultants who dogged their steps under a barrage of slanderous attacks, legal hindrances, court orders, and false reports in the "media" of that era.

Does this sound at all like the era of Cyrus-Trump and his constant battle with the media, rogue intelligence agencies, and efforts to falsely frame or otherwise impeach and remove him from office? Believers in America seemed to think that the restoration of America was a Trump project, as if he alone could reverse the nation's spiritual decline. What we have failed to see is that modern Cyrus rulers are raised up, not to function as spiritual reformers, but to provide a *window of grace* for God's people to do the project assigned to them.

GOD'S BUILDING PROJECT

In a short two-chapter book called Haggai, we discover that the Jewish people also prized peace and prosperity more than the recovery of Jerusalem; they had given up on building God's house. Yet the difficulties they faced were not so hard to overcome that they had to stop the work. Instead, they felt they had done enough for the time being and assumed they had *plenty of time* to finish later.

After sixteen years of no progress, something happened—an economic judgment hit their land. As the devastating setback overtook the people, they discovered that nothing they put their hands to worked. Every endeavor was failing. All the gains they experienced during the project's delay were wiped out. God had a dispute with His people and was sending them a message. To make sure they understood it, He sent them two prophets, one old and one young: Haggai and Zechariah.

While Haggai's record of ministry was just four months long, four months was all that was needed to produce an awakening. His first message rocked them as he related what he heard God tell him: *"This people says, 'The time has not come, the time that the Lord's house should be built.'"*[9] The first

---

9 Haggai 1:2 (NKJV).

word was a rebuke for misunderstanding the urgency of their times. The next word Haggai delivered cut even deeper, accusing Zerubbabel and God's people of living with a double standard. They not only missed the timing of God, they were guilty of using that time for their own personal agendas: *"Is it time for you, yourselves, to dwell in your own 'paneled houses' while My house lies in ruins?"*[10] Paneled houses refers to their own enterprises. They were guilty of being self-absorbed and consumed with building their own economic wellbeing while God's project languished. They were completely ignorant of the hour in which they lived. They were asleep to the significance of their task. They laid a foundation but left God's temple unfinished. To God, the unfinished assignment was unacceptable, and because of this, they were undergoing a national judgement: *"Now this is what the LORD of Hosts says: 'Consider carefully your ways. You have planted much but harvested little. You eat but never have enough. You drink but never have your fill. You put on clothes but never get warm. You earn wages to put into a bag pierced through.... Consider carefully your ways.'"*[11] The prophet's job was now to get the remnant back on track.

MAKING SENSE OF THE SHAKING

As Haggai delivered the Word of the Lord, it hit home:

> *"Go up into the hills, bring down lumber, and build the house, so that I may take pleasure in it and be glorified," says the LORD. "You expected much, but behold, it amounted to little. And what you brought home, I blew away. Why?" declares the LORD of Hosts. "Because My house still lies in ruins, while each of you is busy with his own house. Therefore, on account of you, the heavens have withheld their dew and the earth has withheld its crops. I have summoned a drought on the fields and on the mountains, on the grain, new wine, and oil, and on whatever the ground yields, on man and beast, and on all the labor of your hands."*[12]

The people were in adversity because of their complacency! Their pain was the direct result of their unfinished assignment. *"My house*

---

10 Adapted from Haggai 1:4 (AMP).
11 Haggai 1:5–7 (Berean Study Bible).
12 Adapted from Haggai 1:8–11 (NIV).

still lies in ruins, while each of you is busy with his own house."[13] As a result of their choices, God pronounced a sentence "*on all the labor of your hands.*"[14]

It took them two months to weigh what they were hearing and seeing. What were they working through? Their sin was two-fold:

1. Lack of urgency: They believed they had time to do what they wanted and then come back to the Lord's project. The feeling of "we have time" led to the people in Haggai's day building their own houses and neglecting God's House.

   Many today live under a similar cloud of prophetic confusion. When economic judgment destroyed their harvests, the Jewish people knew God was sending them a message. It has taken us a plague, economic shock, riots, attacks on churches, and the threat of enemies taking over the government just to get our attention.

2. Lack of Dedication: They didn't have a sense of dedication to God's building project. After seventy years in servitude to Babylon and being familiar with submitting to oppressors, they had forgotten their heritage and their identity as God's chosen people. A victim mindset had taken hold, and they turned away from the project they were commissioned to complete. They ignored the prophetic words of God spoken through Isaiah[15] and Jeremiah[16] that the Lord's house would be built, and instead they turned aside to their own projects and built lavish houses for themselves.

Likewise, it can be said that the people of God in the United States think they have more time. Up until the virus lockdown, Christians would tell me that they were not concerned about America because "prophet so and so said Trump would be elected for two terms." On the other side of the ditch, we have many who are convinced it is the last days, and that is why they don't vote. Or on the other side, we have dualists who think

---

13 Haggai 1:9 (Berean Study Bible).
14 Haggai 1:11 (Berean Study Bible).
15 See Isaiah 43:45.
16 See Jeremiah 30:18.

the spirit realm never gets involved with the natural realm and don't care. Yet they both assume that the next event on God's timeline is the rapture.

But the house-building project is so important to the Lord that He tells the people through Haggai that he is going to *"shake everything that can be shaken,"*[17] including heaven and earth and **every nation**.

Both then and now, God has a global house project: *"For this is what the LORD of Hosts says: "'Once more, in a little while, I will shake the heavens and the earth, the sea and the dry land. I will shake all the nations, and they will come with all their treasures, and I will fill this house with glory,' says the LORD of Hosts."*[18]

What is the object of this shaking? Chaos is going to happen, and it will involve shaking the heavens, realigning nations, and filling God's house with glory. Heaven is going to bend every power and every throne to serve the purpose of filling God's house with glory. As the shaking increases, global chaos will shift the affairs of nations one way or another. As a result, God's people and the house of God will experience a corresponding increase in glory and God's presence. We must awaken to the prophetic promises God has given the Church and our nations *even in the midst of shaking* and know that He is with us and has called us to advance!

THE AWAKENING ERROR

There are plenty of people praying for the third great awakening, but what are we being awakened to? What exactly do we mean? Is it a deeper sense of the reality of God, a spiritual encounter, a rededicated life? Or is it something more?

Awakening in a corporate sense and in our private lives often comes on the heels of a major crisis, such as the loss of a job, a family sickness, or a relationship falling out. Any of these things could make us pause to reevaluate our lives. It should drive us to see if we are indeed walking with God.

In the case of Zerubbabel, it was awakening to the fact that their current situation was a heavenly rebuke for the years of disobedience, and the realization that the loss they were experiencing wouldn't stop until they gave God what He wanted—a house for the nation.

---

17 Adapted from Haggai 2:7.
18 Adapted from Haggai 2:6–7.

There is something we cannot afford to miss here: the model for victorious warfare involves the unity of two spheres—marketplace and church—seen in Governor Zerubbabel and Joshua, the priest.

This is how Israel advanced into the Promised Land. The secular warrior Joshua went into battle as Moses, Aaron, and Hur prayed for them. It was a divine partnership. They were on the hill, watching Joshua battle in the valley below. Moses's hands were lifted in spiritual authority as Joshua and the armies of Israel engaged the enemy. When the arms of Moses got weak, the battle reversed for Joshua. When the arms of Moses were held up, Joshua prevailed. It was Arron and Hur who held up the arms of Moses so the battle could be won!

> *Joshua did as Moses had instructed him and fought against the Amalekites, while Moses, Aaron, and Hur went up to the top of the hill. As long as Moses held up his hands, Israel prevailed; but when he lowered them, Amalek prevailed. When Moses' hands grew heavy, they took a stone and put it under him, and he sat on it. Then Aaron and Hur held his hands up, one on each side, so that his hands remained steady until the sun went down.*[19]

Our current model of church leadership is intent on having Joshua and the entire army of Israel standing on the mountain with Moses, experiencing divine visitation, as they pray for the battle. There is no vision for the nation, but there is a vision for revival and the church. The only hope of many is a breakout of revival and the expectation that the world outside will be won over by some sort of mass "evangelism outreach" as a result of a visitation. This is not only a plan that has failed us for the last fifty years, but it is a guaranteed way to lose the battle for the soul of America. To this end, James Davison Hunter makes an important point:

> Imagine, in this regard, a genuine "Third Great Awakening" occurring in America, where half the population is converted to a deep Christian faith. Unless this awakening extended to envelope the cultural gatekeepers, it would have little effect on the character of the symbols that are produced and prevail in public and private culture. And, without a fundamental restructuring of the institutions of cultural formation and transmission in our society—the market,

---

19 Exodus 17:10–12 (Berean Study Bible).

government-sponsored cultural institutions, education and all levels, advertising, entertainment, publishing, and the news media, not to mention church—revival would have a negligible long-term effect on the reconstitution of the culture. Imagine further several social reform movements surrounding, say, educational reform and family policy, becoming very well organized and funded, and on top of this, serious Christians being voted into every major office and appointed to a majority of judgeships. Legislation may be passed and judicial rulings may be properly handed down, but legal and political victories will be short-lived or pyrrhic without the broad-based legitimacy that makes the alternatives seem unthinkable...

This same logic accounts for the contemporary failure of the Christian Right to stop the growth and legitimization of homosexuality, abortion, and pornography, among other concerns. The passion and earnest resolve generated by all such movements may change people and may affect communities and they may, for a time, change laws, **but they generally will not influence the course and direction of the culture as a whole unless they are tied to larger structural changes in the culture.**[20]

Hunter's attention to "broad-based legitimacy" echoes William Wilberforce. Wilberforce was the Christian member of Parliament who led the fight to eradicate slavery in eighteenth-century England. He said that no lasting transformation of culture will succeed without what I describe as a sustained pattern of *public persuasion*. The changes we seek will not be permanent in any awakening or revival without an embracing of Christian thinking that penetrates the populace. Without this, there is no corresponding embrace by elites that occupy the institutional gates of influence. This is how a radical leftist movement in academia has spread through journalism, the media, and Hollywood to gain broad-based consensus in corporations and politics.

The reality is, Christians already outnumber their secular counterparts, and over 60 percent of Americans lean in a conservative direction. In spite of this, we are losing ground. We are being beaten by a smaller number because they are better organized, and they occupy the places of influence.

---

20 James D. Hunter, *To Change the World: The Irony, Tragedy, and Possibility of Christianity in the Late Modern World.* (New York: Oxford University Press, 2010) Emphasis added.

Local churches are just now beginning to realize that the house of God has to have a bigger vision, or it will be shut down by people with a different vision for the role of the Church. Many pastors began to understand the reality of this battle when their own churches were targeted by the government. Governors, mayors, and local officials delivered a surprising series of oppressive illegal edicts.

Did you know in 2020:

- Pastors were arrested for holding church.

- Churchgoers were confined to their houses against their will for attending parking-lot Easter services.[21]

- Churches were threatened with government seizure and bulldozing for daring to open their doors to more than ten people.[22]

- In California singing was banned, and then *all* worship, including Bible studies and fellowship (even in private homes).[23]

Pastor Ché Ahn, of Pasadena, California, knows this threat all too well. He is a recognized apostolic leader with a network of 162 California churches. Ché, like many others, will no longer accept the arbitrary use of power seeking to control the Church, treating it as "nonessential" entertainment. Ché's response to this thought was, "The church has been 'essential' for 2,000 years."[24] When asked why other California churches were not standing in unity with him, he pointed out that the heavy emphasis on the rapture has blurred the ability of believers to see the real battle lines confronting them right now, namely the threat of overreaching government.

---

21 Ladd, Sarah, *Louisville Courier Journal online.* 12 Apr 2020. https://www.courier-journal.com/story/news/2020/04/12/ kentucky-churches-hold-in-person-easter-services-despite-order/5127260002/.

22 "Shining City On A Hill Under Assault." Liberty Council, 5 Aug 2020. https://lc.org/newsroom/details/shining-city-on-a-hill-under-assault.

23 "In-Homel Bible Studies Now Illegal in California?" Liberty Council, 16 Jul 2020. https://faithandlibertydc.org/ detail/20200716inhome-bible-studies-now-illegal-in-california.

24 https://www.cbsnews.com/news/ harvest-rock-church-california-coronavirus-lockdown-violation-services/

To hear Pastor Ché share the harrowing account of what churches are facing and how they are fighting back, go to *FirewallShow.com/Che*.

Regarding the threat of government overreach, the danger is compounded by pastors and elders who see the Church as too holy to mingle itself with "politics." This leads to Francis Shaeffer's warning, "I believe the majority of the silent majority, young and old will sustain the loss of liberties without raising their voices as long as their own life-styles are not threatened."[25] He warned that the greatest threat to Christianity in the West would be the temptation to trade freedom for personal peace and prosperity, but that is the fast track to losing all three: freedom, prosperity, and peace.

I AM WITH YOU

Everything hinges on a change in our understanding of how culture is formed and a corresponding change in *the way the Church engages*. We can no longer assume our rights or freedoms are protected. We are entering church-state tension, much like the early Church; and like the early Church, we need boldness. Where will it come from?

Once Haggai's message hit home, we learn that the presence of God came upon them, and the Lord infused them with His divine energy. "'*I am with you,' says the Lord*." God was telling them not to be intimidated or discouraged. "'*Be strong, Zerubbabel,' says the Lord; 'and be strong, Joshua, son of Jehozadak, the high priest;* **and be strong, all you people of the land,' says the Lord, 'and work for I am with you,'** *says the Lord of hosts*."[26]

"*So the Lord* **stirred up the spirit** *of Zerubbabel the son of Shealtiel governor of Judah,* **and the spirit** *of Joshua the son of Jehozadak, the high priest* **and the spirit of all** *the remnant of the people and they came* **and worked on the house** *of the Lord of hosts their God*."[27] This awakening came in order to accomplish *one* thing—the building of the house of the Lord, a house for the *nation!*

The word *stirred* is the Hebrew word "ur" (pronounced: oor), which means to awaken! The word is used to "stir up, excite, raise up, arouse

---

25 Dabbs, Matt. "Francis Schaeffer on the Politics of Peace and Affluence." Wineskins. wineskins.org, March 29, 2016. http://wineskins.org/2016/03/29/ francis-schaeffer-on-the-politics-and-peace-and-affluence/.

26 Haggai 2:4 (NKJV).

27 Haggai 1:14 (NASB).

to action, to open one's eyes." Occurring nearly seventy-five times in the Old Testament "ur" is used to describe an "eagle stirring up her nest," as in Deuteronomy 32:11, and in Isaiah 50:4 (NKJV) the prophet said, *"He awakens ["ur"] me morning by morning, he awakens my ear to hear."* It's used in Isaiah 45:13 (NIV): *"I will **raise up** ["ur"] Cyrus in my righteousness: I will make all his ways straight. He will rebuild my city and set my exiles free, but not for a price or reward, says the LORD Almighty."* God awakened Cyrus to the role he played in God's prophetic timeline.

The awakening confidence-booster they tapped into was the reality that God played a role in His building project and that His covenant with Moses and the people of Israel was still in effect. God says, *"According to the*

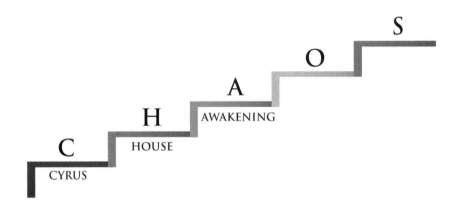

word that I covenanted with you when you came out of Egypt so My Spirit remains among you; do not fear!"[28] God reminded them of their covenant and the promise He gave Moses that through it all, God's presence would remain *strong* among them.

We've looked at the role of the governor and the priest, but what about the prophet? The Lord's words through the prophets are what produced the awakening for Zerubbabel and Joshua. In the era of Cyrus, God is calling for a unique collaboration between the prophetic, priestly, and political leadership in order to see God's will accomplished for the land.

---

28 Haggai 2:5 (NKJV).

God is speaking to prophets to call the modern-day Church to "rise up" and to awaken. It must awaken to the reality that the people are not called to just come to a church building, but we are called to go into all the world around us and be the Church in professions and communities and world systems and structures. We are to become micro-groups: going into school board meetings, executive offices, school halls, state departments, and more! A house for the nation is a Church that engages the Seven Mountains of influence by identifying, supporting, and resourcing the body of Christ located at the front lines of the battle of influence. A house for the nation will require a coming together of many leaders.

What is our task when we meet? We are being asked for a unique collaboration between the "Zerubbabels" in government, the "Joshuas" in the house of God, and the "people" to boldly pursue the building project. Each of us has an assigned area. As a remnant responds to the shaking and goes to work, awakening starts.

The resolution of our global economic shaking, restlessness, and loss of religious freedom—even the threat of losing liberty itself—will not come through revival, awakening, or intense intercession alone. God is saying that the end of the shaking is tied to his original mission; it is tied to the Church being a house for the nations.

As the Chaos Code unfolds, we see that the "H" in Chaos is step number two in the sequence. After a *Cyrus* ruler emerges, a window of grace is initiated where the people of God must build for the Lord what He is asking for—a *house* for the nation. As the sacred books of Haggai, Nehemiah, and Ezra speak to us about the pattern of the Chaos Code, God's people often resist and shrink back from the task of shepherding a nation. As a result, God sends the prophets to correct and then encourage His people, which catalyzes an *awakening*. This step in the Chaos Code is the "A."

The house and the awakening are only half of God's building project. With the first part done, God's next building project in the prophetic timeline was to restore the protective walls and gates of the city. Governor Zerubbabel and the temple priest Joshua, along with a willing remnant, would set up that next phase of the Chaos Code, Nehemiah's project. It would take one team to start it and a second team to bring it to completion.

CHAPTER 3

IT'S A 7M WORLD

"When the solution is simple, God is answering."[1]
—*Albert Einstein*

Zerubbabel's remnant succeeded in building the temple but God's building project was not complete. The once mighty walls and gates that towered over the city 100 years ago were laying in piles of rubble and debris all around the temple. Without walls and gates to keep the people safe, marauding bands of nearby mercenaries were able to raid the city and plunder the people. The walls and gates had to be restored.

The Chaos Code is about to repeat itself, but this time it would be a governor named Nehemiah, a priest named Ezra, and a Cyrus–type ruler named King Artaxerxes. For us modern–day code breakers, the walls and gates of Jerusalem carry a symbolic meaning ; they represent a moral wall protecting culture. Solomon's proverb says: *"Like a city whose walls are broken through is a person who lacks self-control."*[2] A man without self-government is like a defenseless city ; he will spend until bankrupt, eat until obese, and drink until intoxicated. What applies to an individual applies to a nation. Ezekiel 38:11 says , *"I will go up against a land of unwalled villages; I will come against a tranquil people who dwell securely, all of them living without walls or bars*

---

1 "Quote by Albert Einstein." Goodreads, Goodreads Inc., 2020. https://www. goodreads.com/quotes/33577-when-the-solution-is-simple-god-is-answering
2 Proverbs 25:28 (NIV).

or gates—in order to seize the spoil."[3] The Bible is clear—a nation without walls is subject to invasion.

If walls represent the ability of a person or nation to govern itself and protect its people, then gates within the walls represent the key points of entry. The walls of Jerusalem provided a location for community elders, merchants, and judges to meet and decide issues affecting the welfare of the city. Today the gates of entry are places of influence in culture.

America's cultural walls and gates have been crumbling around us. Without intervention we will become an unwalled village that other nations will capitalize on and seize the spoils of our collapse. In the face of this we have the promise Jesus gave us, *"I will build My church and the gates of hell will not prevail against it."*[4] Using the metaphor of gates, Jesus says the counsels of darkness will eventually be thwarted. Their schemes will be overthrown. The gates are not up in the clouds; they are operating over social institutions here on earth.

As we will see in the case of the Israelites, God sent Nehemiah and Ezra to deliver the people from Babylonian captivity and to also bring them a spiritual deliverance from the spirit of Babylon. The root word for "babel" means to confuse, fragment, and disunify.

Today America is under this same Babylonian spirit bent on confusing, fragmenting, and disunifying people. The sacred must be aligned for the secular to be rebuilt. The code tells us that in order to stop the chaos, the *sacred* has to be aligned before the *secular* can be rebuilt. Two primary offices worked together for the restoration of Jerusalem's walls and gates are—Nehemiah *as a representative of government* and Ezra *as the priest.* Together they mobilized a "remnant" to turn things around. All these details are part of the code in our day. Phase two of God's building project will have the same combination of a governor named Nehemiah and priest named Ezra.

THE NEHEMIAH PROJECT

The decree of Cyrus was in effect long after his administration turned over to his successor. The next central character in the code is Nehemiah , who was the trusted cupbearer to King Artaxerxes. By occupation, a cupbearer

3 Ezekiel 38:11 (Berean Study Bible).
4 Matthew 16:18 (ESV).

is both a conversational companion and chief of security for royalty, as poison would be the number one way for a rival to get access to the throne. This was the man who tasted the king's food and drink. Nehemiah was promoted to a place of influence because, like Esther, he would be used for the welfare of God's people.

One day the brother of Nehemiah, Hanani, and other men of Judah were visiting him in Persia. They told him how the Jews in Jerusalem were being bullied and harassed by other inhabitants of their homeland. They said, *"The remnant who survived the exile are there in the province, in great trouble and disgrace. The wall of Jerusalem is broken down, and its gates are burned with fire."*[5] The temple was completed, but without walls and gates, they were prey to foreign tribes. They lived under constant threat of attack and plunder by vicious neighbors.

When Nehemiah heard the report, he was deeply troubled. He was so disturbed by the news, he wept and mourned for days, fasting and praying before God. He knew he had to say something to the king on behalf of his people so he prayed,

> *O LORD, God of heaven, the great and awesome God who keeps His covenant of loving devotion with those who love Him and keep His commandments, let Your eyes be open and Your ears attentive to hear the prayer that I, Your servant, now pray before You day and night for Your servants, the Israelites.*
>
> *I confess the sins that we Israelites have committed against You. Both I and my father's house have sinned. We have behaved corruptly against You and have not kept the commandments, statutes, and ordinances that You gave Your servant Moses.*
>
> *Remember, I pray, the word that You commanded Your servant Moses when You said, "'f you are unfaithful, I will scatter you among the nations, but if you return to Me and keep and practice My commandments, then even if your exiles have been banished to the farthest horizon, I will gather them from there and bring them to the place I have chosen as a dwelling for My Name."*
>
> *They are Your servants and Your people. You redeemed them by Your great power and mighty hand. O Lord, may Your ear be attentive to*

---

5 Nehemiah 1:3 (Berean Study Bible).

my prayer and to the prayers of Your servants who delight to revere Your name. Give Your servant success this day, I pray, and grant him mercy in the sight of this man.[6]

The next time Nehemiah saw the king, he could not hide his distress. Upon seeing Nehemiah, the king made him divulge what was bothering him. Nehemiah unburdened his thoughts about his city lying in ruins and its gates burned. In a moment of profound favor, Artaxerxes I was moved by his cupbearer's sorrow. He authorized Nehemiah to return to Jerusalem and to build the walls of the city.

This decision would be the equivalent of authorizing a conquered territory to rearm themselves. The request he made was massive. Nehemiah asked for papers to be drawn up that gave him safe passage through the lands and the resources he would need to rebuild the walls and gates. Artaxerxes I then issued the *"letters to the governors of Syria and Palestine and especially to Asaph, the keeper of the king's forest, ordering him to supply timber for the wall, the fortress, and the temple."*[7] This endeavor was going to be costly to the king's treasury. For the duration of this assignment, Nehemiah was promoted to the status of governor. God gave Nehemiah favor, funding, and authority, the three things he would need to rebuild the walls and gates of Zion.

Armed with these credentials, he acquired the resources he needed and set off for Jerusalem. When he arrived, the first thing he did was slip out under the cover of night to conduct a survey of the broken-down walls and the gates. When he returned, he gathered the people, priests, nobles, officials, and other workers and said to them, *"You see the trouble we are in. Jerusalem lies in ruins, and its gates have been burned down. Come, let us rebuild the wall of Jerusalem, so that we will no longer be a disgrace."*[8] He also told them about the gracious hand of God upon him and what the king had done for him. At that report, the people said *"Let us start rebuilding,"* and they *"set their hands"*[9] immediately to the work. As with Zerubbabel, once the leader was in place, the people responded.

---

6 Nehemiah 1:5–11 (Berean Study Bible).
7 Adapted from Nehemiah 2:7–8.
8 Nehemiah 2:17 (Berean Study Bible).
9 Nehemiah 2:18 (Berean Study Bible).

Not everyone was pleased to see Nehemiah helping the Jews. The Bible says that when *"Sanballat the Horonite and Tobiah the Ammonite official heard about this, they were deeply disturbed that someone had come to seek the well-being of the Israelites."*[10] Sanballat and the others ridiculed the work of the Israelites, telling them the size of the project was too vast to complete because there was too much rubble to clear. He ridiculed them as being small and weak, he said they wouldn't be able to do this by themselves, he mocked them for working hard, and he criticized the resources they had to work with. If Nehemiah was going to rebuild the walls and gates, he had to overcome some major problems that Sanballat was stirring up in the people.

YOU FIGHT FOR YOUR FAMILY

The people began to experience deep discouragement because of Sanballat's voice. Nehemiah had powerful enemies; and the Jewish people, without walls of protection, were fearful of being singled out for destruction. He needed the people to move en masse, *as one* people.

They prayed a strong prayer to God, *"Hear us, O God, for we are despised. Turn their scorn back upon their own heads, and let them be taken as plunder to a land of captivity. Do not cover up their iniquity or let their sin be blotted out from Your sight, for they have provoked the builders."*[11] After that they pressed even harder into rebuilding the wall, *"until all of it was joined together up to half its height."* Again the Bible says, *"for the people had a mind to work."*[12]

Sanballat became all the more furious that the people made progress as the wall was being restored and the gaps were being closed. He and the others were so enraged they actually *"conspired to come and fight against Jerusalem and create a hindrance."*[13] They threatened to kill the Jews and put an end to their work.

While this violent conspiracy was hatching, the people were beginning to grow weary with the psychological bombardment. Nehemiah records them as saying, *"The strength of the laborer fails, and there is so much rubble that we will never be able to rebuild the wall."*[14] Israelites who lived in

---

10 Nehemiah 2:10 (Berean Study Bible).
11 Nehemiah 4:4–5 (Berean Study Bible).
12 Nehemiah 4:6 (Berean Study Bible).
13 Nehemiah 4:8 (Berean Study Bible).
14 Nehemiah 4:10 (Berean Study Bible).

the area overheard details of Sanballat's plot and warned Nehemiah that attacks were imminent and would come from every angle. To continue the work, these weary people would need dynamic leadership and a winning strategy in order to defend what they had been called to.

These same feelings of discouragement, weariness, fear, and even physical threat plague many Christian conservatives today. I can think of no other recent news story that drives home this point more soberly than the Tulsa Trump rally in May of 2020. Tulsa, one of the most reliably Christian conservative cities in America, was the location of Trump's first rally after the COVID-19 pandemic lockdowns. The Tulsa Bank of Oklahoma (BOK) stadium holds just over 19,000 people and had projections of not just being sold out, but also having half a million people outside. The registration numbers were so high because tech savvy leftists launched a campaign to swamp the rally with fake attendees. Unfortunately for the Trump team, only about 6,000 supporters showed up—but why? Conservatives did not attend because in one way or another they were manipulated, intimidated, and discouraged; they feared catching the coronavirus and being physically attacked by aggressive BLM protesters and Antifa. The devil isn't creative in how he resists the saints of God. It is always the same pattern: He will say whatever he can to discourage you from showing up. If that doesn't work, he will threaten you and your family with physical violence to stop you from showing up. This is not new. In response to Paul's ministry triumphs in Thessalonica, his enemies gathered a mob of the worst people they could locate. These men were "**lewd**" (wicked), but to make it worse, they were "of the **baser sort**" (the worst of the worst!). This was the mob that caused riots wherever Paul had a ministry breakthrough.[15]

Christian conservatives have started to let the "Sanballats" of today work their way into our thinking; they have discouraged rebuilding the moral wall that surrounds our nation. It feels like the project is too large, the resources are so meager, and our numbers are so small. Why even try?

In Nehemiah's case, to overcome his enemies, he stopped the work and assembled the people to fight. He records his strategy, *"I stationed men behind the lowest sections of the wall, at the vulnerable areas. I stationed them with their families with their swords, spears, and bows."*[16] Notice Nehemiah stationed the

---

15 Adapted from Acts 17:5 (KJV).
16 Nehemiah 4:13 (Berean Study Bible).

people in the vulnerable areas of the wall; he didn't station them everywhere. I think today the Church is avoiding the areas of weakness in the deteriorating moral wall of our nation. We need to move toward the vulnerabilities, armed to defend issues that are crumbling like sanctity of life and marriage.

Also, Nehemiah stationed people by family. Each household would be most motivated to defend the area of the wall adjacent to where they lived. He writes, *"And I looked, and arose and said to the nobles, to the leaders, and to the rest of the people, 'Do not be afraid of them. Remember the Lord, great and awesome, and fight for your brethren, your sons, your daughters, your wives and your houses."*[17]

I want you to see that the future of your family must be the ultimate cause of alarm to rebuild the walls of today's culture. Those of us who are older have lived our lives in peace, but what future are we sending our children into? We have shut our ears to the attacks conservative youth have been left exposed to on campuses, and the savaging they endure when campus radicals and Internet mobs attack. They will be mocked, robbed of employment, saddled with an impossible national debt, and forced to hide their faith in shame or stand up to potential violence in the cultural hell we have allowed to be created around them.

Most importantly, your example means something. If you fail to stand and do what is required, what sort of Christian legacy are you leaving them? Will they remember you as someone who lived your faith and fought for them and their future? Or will they remember you as someone who lived a small life, hiding as long as possible while cowering from the coming battle? As Nehemiah charged the people of his day, the same words challenge us today: *"Remember the Lord, great and awesome, and fight for your brethren, your sons, your daughters, your wives and your houses!"*[18]

Upon seeing that the Jews had turned into a formidable enemy, Sanballat realized that his plan was ruined. The Israelites now knew they had to fight as they built. They learned how to go on offense and defense. From that day on, *"half of my servants did the work while the other half held spears, shields, bows, and armor."*[19] The laborers carried the building materials to

---

17 Nehemiah 4:14 (NKJV).
18 Nehemiah 4:14 (NKJV).
19 Nehemiah 4:16 (Berean Study Bible).

work in one hand and held a weapon with the other; each of the builders worked with his sword strapped to his side.

The aggressive, intimidating tactics of Antifa and BLM are the same spirit that was unleashed against the Hebrews as they rebuilt their temple and the walls. The awareness we need to have is that, like the Israelites, we must learn to defend our cultural worldview and not apologize for it. The question we face is, "Are we willing to face these risks in order to leave something better behind for our children?" If we don't, today's moral wall will continue to collapse and God's building project will be left for another generation, in a worse state than it is in now.

WHO WILL SUMMON THE MIGHTY MEN?

One other challenge Nehemiah faced was the ability to mobilize everyone quickly in case of an attack. They needed to be able to swarm "as one man" against any point of attack. To fix this Nehemiah said, *"'The work is great and extensive, and we are separated far from one another on the wall. Wherever you hear the sound of the trumpet, rally to us there. Our God will fight for us.'"*[20]

Likewise today, this absence of unity compromises our ability to stand en masse against attacks on individual businesses, houses of worship, or political allies. This has become one of our greatest weaknesses. There is **no centralized, unifying trumpet call.** The closest thing we have to consistent messaging and protection (for the moment) is a besieged president. Add a few courageous voices in the Republican Party, a half dozen overworked Christian legal organizations, and a few Washington-based Christian 501c4s with mailing lists, and that is our collective trumpet. Does this really express the combined power and influence of 100 million or even 50 million Christians? The Church in America will now have to form a new more muscular and cohesive mechanism to sound the trumpet and show up at the point where the battle is decisive.

In my first meeting with Donald Trump before he was president, he said, *"Christians are the biggest single demographic in America. There's nothing you can't do if you pull together, but that's not my job—but it should be somebody*

---

20 Nehemiah 4:19–20 (Berean Study Bible).

else's. Someone needs to get you guys together." He has more faith in the Church than the Church has in itself.

At some point, there will need to be a convening of the most influential men and women in the Church. This joint meeting needs leaders in the marketplace and in government as well. We must learn to move as one if we are going to rebuild the moral wall and occupy the gates of nations.

Church convenings have happened in the past. In AD 48, a gathering of all the elders and the apostles took place to discuss whether the early Church should accept Gentiles into the movement. The fact that these were all leaders in the early Church, many of whom had heard Jesus, did not mean they were in unity. To the contrary, the Bible says, *"And when there had been much dispute"*[21] Peter rose up to point out that God had chosen him to be the first to go to the Gentiles. The Church has often been required to come together, such as the Council of Nicaeain AD 325 to settle important issues.

The point is, today **we need another convening** if we are to navigate against a vastly more unified Sanballat. There will be disagreement, just as there has been in the past; but if we can agree and stand together, we can advance *as one.* What God is speaking to the Church is significant, and unfortunately we are like the Jews in Nehemiah's project—the wall is vast and we are spread out and disconnected from each other.

IT'S A 7M™ WORLD

Within the cultural wall that surrounds our nation, there are seven primary gates of influence where decisions are made that affect our lives. I see these gates like all ancient strongholds, situated on top of the high places of cultural influence. I call these high places the Seven Mountains of culture. These mountains are the mission fields. They shape and disciple nations. It is a 7M world. Earthly mountains have a narrow top and a broad base; so do the mountains of culture. The tops of mountains are made up of a remnant of *gatekeeper elites,* relatively small groups that occupy the high places of influence. They are supported by dense, overlapping networks of gatekeeper elites. They influence decisions on everything from what song will be popular this week to what stories play in the media, and what laws will get passed.

---

21 Acts 15:7 (NKJV).

The left has increasingly influenced and shaped these mountains. The first description I heard about these high leverage points of influence was from Loren Cunningham who described them appropriately as the "mind molders of culture." Bill Bright had also come up with seven areas of influence that he referred to as world kingdoms. I saw these concepts and created a picture that reflects how these spheres are organized as a descending hierarchy of influence, broad at the bottom yet dominated at the top.

These seven mountains are:

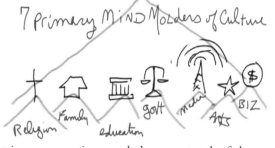

1. Church
2. Family
3. Education
4. Big Government
5. Big Media
6. Big Entertainment
7. Big Business

These mountains exist in every nation, and the sum total of these mountains determines whether the nation is oppressed under the heel of a hostile government or whether it's free, prosperous, and blessed. One of the best teachings I have ever done on the Seven Mountains was at the Value Voters Summit; if you ever want to watch this illustration be brought to life, visit godschaoscode.com/7m. The average Christian doesn't recognize that he or she has a commission and anointing as God's ambassador in these mountains and at the gates. Most Christians believe they're just to be witnesses, and they defer to the clergy as the anointed ones who must save culture. The Church sees itself as separate from the battles for culture and seeks to avoid controversy. Many Christians don't see that the Church has checked out of the cultural battle; and in their sphere, they are the anointed guardians of the gates that hell seeks to occupy.

In all the mountains, the higher up you go and the more involved you are, the more prestige, credibility, and influence you possess. This is where we as the Church must begin to penetrate with our own cohorts of awakened Christians. We are the people who are supposed to protect the territory we are assigned to by "occupying" ground until He comes.

THE FEAST OF THE OPEN BOOK

In all of Nehemiah's reforms, he was assisted by Ezra, who had gone up to Jerusalem thirteen years before Nehemiah. **Ezra** was a senior rabbi and reformer who reeducated the returned Jewish community on the teachings of the Torah. While Nehemiah rebuilt in the civic arena, Ezra *rebuilt the people of God.*

Once the walls and gates were restored, the people gathered together "as one man" in the open square, and they asked Ezra to read the Book of the Law of Moses. Nehemiah tells us that, "*On the first day of the seventh month, Ezra the priest brought the Law before the assembly of men and women and all who could listen and understand. So Ezra read it aloud from daybreak until noon.*"[22] This took place during the Feast of Tabernacles, a feast that is pregnant with prophetic meaning as it corresponds to a promised outpouring of God in the end of the age. It should be noted that this feast followed Nehemiah's reforms. With the assistance of thirteen Levites, Ezra taught and his team mingled with the people in order to give them a clear understanding, "*So they read from the Book of the Law of God, explaining it and giving insight, so that the people could understand what was being read. Nehemiah the governor, Ezra the priest and scribe, and the Levites who were instructing the people said to all of them, 'This day is holy to the LORD your God. Do not mourn or weep.' For all the people were weeping as they heard the words of the Law.*"[23]

As the people understood the meaning of the words it produced a conviction, a deep piercing of the heart. In response to this, Nehemiah exhorted the people and said, "*Go your way, eat the fat, drink the sweet, and send portions to those for whom nothing is prepared; for this day is holy to our Lord. Do not sorrow, for the joy of the LORD is your strength.*"[24]

During the first day of reading, the people and Ezra discovered that it was, in fact, the time of the Feast of Tabernacles. This feast was celebrated annually during the harvest season in Israel. It was one of three feasts Moses commanded the Jewish people to observe. The primary Jewish feasts are Passover, Pentecost, and Tabernacles. Two of these have been fulfilled and experienced by the Church:

---

22 Nehemiah 8:2 (Berean Study Bible).
23 Nehemiah 8:8–9 (Berean Study Bible).
24 Nehemiah 8:10 (NKJV).

- **Passover** occurred at the crucifixion of Jesus. Salvation by the blood of the lamb was fulfilled in Passover.

- **Pentecost** was the feast celebrated fifty days following Passover. Jesus appeared to the disciples for forty days and instructed them to wait the next ten days for the coming *"enduement of power from on high"*[25] that occurred on Pentecost. This feast corresponded with the beginning of the harvest season for Israel. It was on this day that the first harvest of 3,000 souls were saved through the preaching of Peter, and the New Testament Church was formed.

- **The Feast of Tabernacles is yet** to be fulfilled. It is most interesting that this coming feast is brought into light in the books of Ezra and Nehemiah. There is one reference to Jesus and Tabernacles in the gospels. John records that Jesus went into the feast in a covert manner, with no fanfare; then suddenly in the middle of it, He rose and began to teach. Based on Ezra and Nehemiah, this end-time feast is a time of both conviction and great joy, because **the book is opened and the meaning of the words are suddenly and powerfully understood**. This is a feast of revelation and harvest.

The Feast of Tabernacles is the *feast of the open book* and the feast of the great final harvest. What does this have to do with the Chaos Code? The Code reveals a pattern to awakening and outpouring. The awakening we are asking for, praying for, and believing God for only comes after the house of God has been built, the walls fortified, and the gates occupied. In the Chaos Code, there are two times the people experienced awakening:

- First, when they embraced God's building project

- Second, when they embraced God's Word

Our awakening is stalled because we are out of sync with the Chaos Code. We haven't completed (or even started) God's building project. What good does it do to have an awakening if we are not going to experience lasting cultural change? What happens to Christians in China when they experience revival but are then rounded up and sent to "reeducation"

---

25 Adapted from Luke 24:49.

camps? If we have an outpouring in America and God's presence shows up but we have failed to occupy the gates of influence, how long will it be before such meetings are opposed, monitored, and disbanded?

We first need to rebuild the house, then the walls, and finally occupy the gates. Then we will experience the lasting outpouring we desire and turn back to the Word of God. The question before us is whether we will answer God's call to build by defending against and resisting those who would seek to discourage us from the work.

Remember, Jesus has promised us that, "*I will build My church and the gates of hell will not prevail against it.*"[26] The gates of hell are the counsels of darkness aligning themselves with earthly rulers in order to exercise their will on the earth. Think about that.

There are times that we put too much of an emphasis on our battle with spiritual forces and miss the fact that this conflict is working through human agency. Remember Paul writes in Ephesians 6:12, "*For we wrestle not against flesh and blood, but against principalities, against powers, against the rulers of the darkness of this world, against spiritual wickedness in high places.*"[27] But this verse does not say we should ignore human agency; it merely tells us we are called to confront the spiritual forces working through people and systems. Earlier in Ephesians, Paul clarifies that we wrestle with "*the prince of the power of the air, the spirit that now works in the children of disobedience.*"[28]

THE FEAST OF TABERNACLES IS THE FEAST OF THE OPEN BOOK AND THE FEAST OF THE GREAT FINAL HARVEST.

The gates of hell are the counsels of darkness that influence people to materialize hell on earth. These agendas are worked out through earthly rulers and those who are empowered at the gates of influence. For this reason we see why God has called His people to envision their role as a city set on a hill. They are called to be the "*head and not the tail, above and not beneath.*"[29] Christian influence and thought are needed in the high places

---

26 Matthew 16:18 (NHEB).
27 Ephesians 6:12 (KJV).
28 Ephesians 2:2 (NKJV).
29 Adapted from Deuteronomy 28:13 (ISV).

of the mountains. This is where salt and light are most effective. It is the history of the Reformation in Europe and the Great Awakening's influence in America. The call is to *"rule in the midst of thine enemies"*[30] as opposed to withdrawing to a safe distance.

THE KEY THAT UNLOCKS NATIONS

The Church was given powerful keys of authority to bind and to loose; they are called *"the keys of the kingdom."*[31] These are the tools we use to fulfill Jesus's prayer, *"Thy will be done on earth as it is in heaven."*[32] It might be helpful to see that the Church is *not* the kingdom. The Church has been given the keys of the kingdom.

This is an important distinction, because what happens when the Church is placed in a position to rule over all Seven Mountains? We saw that experiment in the dark ages, and it did not end well. In fact, it was a disaster. The Church has its proper sphere, and it is sovereign and stands apart, but is not disconnected. The Church makes disciples. The disciples in each sphere know best how to advance righteousness within their domain. This is the key to discipling nations.

The model of Ezra and Nehemiah is what we are after. Church leaders need to train and equip disciples to go into their sphere of influence and be a witness, an influence, an agent to unlock the kingdom. The greatest gift modern-day Ezras offer is their ability to teach God's people the Word, instruct them on how to hear God's voice, and demonstrate how to walk with Him. They ground people in their assignment to be disciples of Christ. The disciples bring their salt and light into culture. *They* become the wall and occupy the gates.

We should teach Christians how to unite and function as a fellowship, praying about issues on the front line of their sphere of influence. By focusing inward instead of outward, the average church is seeking to attract and assimilate businesspeople, rather than apostolically activate and send people into the Seven Mountains.

---

30 Adapted from Psalm 110:2 (KJV).
31 See Matthew 16:19.
32 Adapted from Matthew 6:10 (KJV).

We need Ezras to arise and work alongside the Nehemiahs engaged in the front-line battles at the gates. The Church is the authorized agent of heaven that has been equipped with keys that unlock the kingdom on the earth. All it takes are two or more gathered together in the name of Jesus. That's the beginning of occupying your sphere.

It would be helpful here to ask, what exactly does the kingdom look like? We know that the kingdom is the rule of Jesus, but how do we make this something we can observe? My favorite description of this came from Pastor Creflo Dollar of Creflo Dollar Ministries in Atlanta, Georgia. He said, "The kingdom of God is simply God's way of doing things."[33] So in the financial arena, we look at kingdom finance, or "God's way" of doing finances. In marriage, we look at God's Word on relationships. The Bible covers all aspects of life. True disciples should be the true innovators, leaders, and solution finders in every sphere. That is how we fulfill the promise given by God that we would be the *"head and not the tail, above and not beneath."*[34] Where is the best place to unlock all of that authority? At the gates of influence, on top of the Seven Mountains. If we don't advocate for "God's way of doing things" we will end up with impractical and even dangerous ways of doing things.

WHEN KINGDOMS COLLIDE

If God has a way of doing things, then so does the devil. Make no mistake, these two kingdoms are contending for rulership on the earth; and when you do not occupy what was assigned to you, it will be occupied by the devil and used against you. For some reason, the Church has decided that Jesus does not have jurisdiction on the earth until He returns. We pray *"Thy kingdom come, thy will be done on earth"*[35] but can't agree on how it shows up. The truth is we have more faith for the antichrist to manifest than the Lord Jesus Christ. Over the last fifty years, this theology has baptized us into an eschatology of cultural passivity, escapism, and defeat.

---

33 Creflo Dollar, "Prosperity God's Way." Creflo Dollar Ministries, 17 July 2020.
    https://www.creflodollarministries.org/Bible-Study/Articles/Prosperity-Gods-Way
34 Deuteronomy 28:13 (ISV).
35 Matthew 6:10 (KJV).

If you think Jesus can't rule on the earth until His return, then ask yourself this: Why did He tell us that, *"All authority in heaven and on earth* **has been** *given to Me. Therefore* **go** *and make disciples of* **all nations**."[36] He told us to go because Jesus, not the devil, now has all authority. He has commissioned you with all authority to *go*. If you and I don't go, the kingdom doesn't come.

Why has He given us all this authority? Is it so we can have a better, happier life? So we can achieve the goals on our vision boards? Jesus gave this authority so that His message would impact nations before He returns. Our vision is too small. The call to go make disciples of nations has often been read as *"go make disciples* **in** *all the nations."* The verse, however, points to discipling nations, not individuals. Not all nations will respond, but the promise holds out that nations can, and should be discipled.

In Psalm 2:8, God the Father is speaking to the Son at the resurrection, saying: *"Ask of Me, and I will give You The nations for Your inheritance, And the ends of the earth for Your possession."*[37] The inheritance of Jesus will be the nations of the earth. Consider this: soul winning will end and so will revivals, but nations and the "glory of nations" go on into eternity.

Our failure to shape the countries we live in stems from our ignorance of what this cultural battle entailed and our indifference or confusion about seeing it done. We have not only failed to keep our nations; we have failed to steward Christ's inheritance. We have not yet fully realized that nations have their own destiny and will one day be presented to the Lord. Suffice it to say, many believers have no vision for seeing nations or cities converted and discipled. That is tragic, because the devil thinks in terms of nations and cities, and he gets them through corrupt politicians and backroom business deals.

A STEADY CURRENT OF DIVINE POWER

The task ahead of us seems insurmountable. The rubble of our cultural walls and gates lies around us. When you add in the devil's "Sanballat-

36 Matthew 28:18–19 (NIV).
37 Psalm 2:8 (NKJV)

like" threats, weariness for many sets in. The work of rebuilding the gates, walls, and house will require God's supernatural grace. Most define this word as "God's unmerited favor," but this is inaccurate. Grace is better understood as a steady current of divine power. Paul said *"But by the grace of God I am what I am, and His grace to me was not in vain. No, I worked harder than all of them—yet not I, but the grace of God that was with me."*[38] It was the power of a divine enablement that was working with him, and that power is called grace.

Let's not forget about Haggai's younger prophetic partner, Zechariah. One of the most quoted Old Testament verses in reference to the work of the Holy Spirit is Zechariah 4:6. In this verse Zechariah prophesied to Zerubbabel that his assignment would be accomplished **"Not by might, nor by power, but by My Spirit says the Lord of Hosts**.*"*[39] There would be great obstacles in his way but he was told, **"Who are you great mountain? Before Zerubbabel you shall become a plain! And he shall bring the capstone with shouts of Grace, Grace to it.**"[40]

God's Church, His city, and the walls and gates must be built and sustained, not by wealth, human strength, or even our own virtue, but *"by My Spirit."*

For those of you who aren't discouraged by the task set before us, but have become discouraged by lies like, "God could never use me; I have messed up too much ," the prophet Zechariah also has a word for you. It is the same word he gave the priest, Joshua, who labored alongside Zerubbabel. The prophet was shown a vision of Joshua as Satan appeared in the form of an accuser opposing him. Joshua's garments were filthy, but the Lord put rich apparel on him and invited him to walk in heavenly realms, where angelic courts take place, and to put his authority to use. Likewise, you too will have moments when you will need to draw upon supernatural grace and divine righteousness for the task in front of us.

---

38 1 Corinthians 15:10 (Berean Study Bible).
39 Zechariah 4:6 (NKJV).
40 Adapted from Zechariah 4:7 (NKJV).

GREAT COMMISSION OR DECOMMISSION?

We are in a moment of sober redefinition regarding the role of the Christian community in America—how it mobilizes, where it shows up, and what it does. I remember Governor Mike Huckabee sharing that a great battleship is "commissioned" by the Navy for service, and when that ship is no longer useful, the navy declares it "decommissioned." The churches and ministries that fail to rise up to answer the Great Commission will at some point be decommissioned. This is the moment for the rearmament of the Church to turn our cruise ship into a battleship as we face a conflict with the forces of darkness at the gates of influence in media, education, and big government.

Mario Murillo reminds us that, "We did not pick this fight. They brought the fight to us. We didn't wander into politics; they invaded the Church. They jumped the fence into our yard. We did not spiritualize politics. They politicized spirituality. They wandered into our lane, ordering us to violate our conscience and worse—to disobey God."[41]

This is the trumpet call to *occupy* the gates and breaches in the wall. This rallying cry to advance from the temple to the gates is the "O" in the Chaos Code. As we move outward to where the battle is raging, we get closer to standing in the gap where the wall is weak. We are contending for Jesus's inheritance, the sheep nations of the earth.

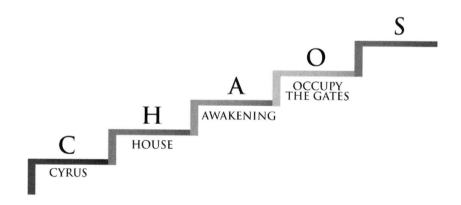

S
O — OCCUPY THE GATES
A — AWAKENING
H — HOUSE
C — CYRUS

---

41 Mario Murillo, Vessels of Fire and Glory (Shippensburg, PA: Destiny Image Publishers, Inc, 2019), 75

CHAPTER 4

SHEEP NATIONS RISING!

"If the idea is not at first absurd, then there is no hope for it"[1]
—*Albert Einstein*

Somewhere in the midst of America's freedom and flourishing, the Church ceased to occupy the land that it was promised and turned the Lion of the Tribe of Judah into a domesticated house pet, meeting in local churches and hotel ballrooms. In truth, the Christian's call to "make disciples of nations" has been reduced to sermons on how to get saved, get along, and live a happy life.

Some people think the Bible has nothing to say regarding the cultural issues we face, but Jesus says the opposite. When tempted by Satan in the wilderness, Jesus said, *"Man shall not live by bread alone but by every word that proceeds from the mouth of God."*[2] The term *man* could be extrapolated to: all mankind—sinners, saints, communists, Democrats, Republicans, agnostics, and atheists—shall all live by every word that proceeds from the mouth of God. The Bible covers everything, and where it doesn't with specificity, it offers the relevant principles that do apply.

---

1 "Quotes By Albert Einstein." IMDb, 2020. https://m.imdb.com/name/nm0251868/quotes.
2 Matthew 4:4 (NKJV).

There are obviously many in God's Church who want to get involved in shaping culture; they're just not sure what to do because they aren't being instructed. Decent Christians can be very confused on the issues, and many preachers only make it worse by their silence on cultural topics. Some even make it worse with their support of progressive talking points.

In an article from Wallbuilders, "What God's People Want to Know," George Barna shared results from a survey he had done in 2015 among 2,868 spiritually active Christians who were politically conservative or moderate. He wanted to determine what role Christian churches played in recent elections, what issues pastors were most likely to consider important in the 2016 election, and what kind of issues–related teaching Christians wanted from their churches during that election cycle.

Here's what he discovered: "Spiritually active Christians who hold politically conservative views believe that churches should be more involved in the political process. In particular, they are eager for their pastors to teach them what the Bible says about today's social and political issues."[3]

In fact, a majority of the churchgoers surveyed said it is *extremely* or *very important* for their church to teach them biblical truths related to each of the twenty–two different issues studied in this research![4] If we want to shift culture and save our nation, it starts by helping believers be confident on how to address issues. Then we can update our paradigm from bigger churches and more evangelism to reforming systems and nations.

Unfortunately, the left has been diligent in their own indoctrination campaign, which makes the Church's cultural illiteracy more dangerous. The left made it their goal to gain influence, and that's exactly what they have done.

---

3 George Barna, "What God's People Want to Know." *WallBuilders*, 2018, https://wallbuilders.com/gods-people-want-know/#.

4 George Barna, "What God's People Want to Know." *WallBuilders*, 2018, https://wallbuilders.com/gods-people-want-know/#.

SHEEP NATIONS RISING![5]

Issue	Extremely	Very
Abortion	74%	20%
Religious persecution/liberty	64	26
Sexual identity	59	27
Cultural restoration	56	30
Poverty	55	31
Israel	56	26
Christian heritage	49	33
Role of government	46	33
Bioethics	51	27
Self-governance	44	34
Church in politics/government	43	33
Islam	45	29
Media	40	32
Senior citizens	36	36
Patriotism	40	31
Public school education	40	32
Government authority	42	29
Political participation	38	32
War	33	36
Rule of law	35	32
Civil disobedience	31	35
Government accountability	25	27

THE LOST GOSPEL OF THE KINGDOM

Christians often live in a split universe, withdrawing from all contact with the world in the quest for an exclusively spiritual life. Ironically, this is the fast track to missing the call of God on your life. Instead of acquiring skills and knowledge that make you promotable into areas of influence and opportunity, you end up participating in a much smaller field of global activity. This is probably implied by the verse *"Those who go down to the sea*

5 George Barna, "What God's People Want to Know." *WallBuilders*, 2018, https://wallbuilders.com/gods-people-want-know/#.

in ships, Who do business on great waters; They have seen the works of the Lord, and His wonders in the deep."[6]

I have done that myself, withdrawing from what I perceived to be worldly or secular pursuits. I was in my twenties as a senior manager in a Fortune 500 oil company with headquarters fifty minutes outside of Manhattan, New York. I left those corporate corridors in order to dedicate myself to the "call of God." The only door that opened was a church where I volunteered to play keyboards as a worship leader. It was a new church, starting out over an auto body shop in a humble part of town in Fort Washington, near Philadelphia. We called it the Upper Room, which worked fine in the summer; but in the winter, the garage on the first floor would close its doors and turn on the cars and asphyxiate all of us in the "Upper Room."

It all eventually worked out for me; as it turns out, I was actually called to do what I do. Unfortunately, this "dualism" is a common error in the Christian community. It has robbed many believers of the destiny they seek to fulfill because they don't understand that the call to go into "all the world" is not just a geographic call to missionaries, but a vocational call to go into all the systems of this world, to *"do business on great waters."*

The reality is that God has called only "some" to full-time ministry: "God gave *some* apostles, *some* prophets, *some* evangelists, *some* pastors and teachers."[7] No matter how you define "some" it means that *most* are not called to seek full-time vocations in traditional ministry. By Old Testament standards, only 10 percent of the tribes were employed in the Levitical workforce, all making a livelihood connected to the temple. The rest of the 90 percent of Israel were to go forth in their vocations and influence the territory around them. Dualistic Christians can only see the world as spiritual or secular. For us, our imagination is limited to resolving every issue by more prayer and revival. The thinking is that if everybody got saved and went to church, we wouldn't have riots.

The error is costly, producing a hyper focus on church at the expense of the rest of the mandate given to cultivate and disciple nations. This error is best highlighted by missionary Landa Cope when she asked God why Africa, after two hundred years of concentrated missions effort on

---

6 Psalm 107:23–24 (NKJV).

7 Adapted from Ephesians 4:11–16.

the continent, was still riddled with poverty, disease, violence, corruption, injustice, and chaos. God's answer to her was:

> *The devastation you see is the fruit of preaching salvation alone,*
> *without the rest of the biblical message...You may ask, What could*
> *possibly be the problem with the gospel of salvation? The answer to that,*
> *Nothing! There is nothing wrong with the salvation part of the gospel*
> *message we preach today. But as evangelicals, we talk almost exclusively*
> *about the salvation message, being born again, born again believers, born*
> *again churches, and the new birth as though the initial experience of*
> *salvation is the only message.* [8]

Jesus never referred to the gospel of salvation. Jesus taught the gospel of the kingdom: salvation and the truth as it applies to work, money, relationships, justice, and moral choices impacting every dimension of life. The gospel of the kingdom is the full exploration of God's way of doing things. A believer is called to be baptized and immersed in this teaching of Jesus. How does this contrast with more than 150 years of missionary and evangelical work dominated by this concept of salvation as the measure of success?

The first-century Church "filled Jerusalem" with their teaching, and in 300 years dominated the Roman Empire—the same empire that killed many of the apostles. These Christians laid a foundation beneath Western European countries that made them the most prosperous nations in the world. Cope says, "The message that reformed Western cultures and built nations on solidly Christian values was not the gospel of salvation, but the gospel of the kingdom—including salvation."[9] Remember, the message of the kingdom is simply, "God's way of doing things." These truths, when practiced, produce results. Cope's insights continue:

> *The result of a diminished and split gospel is clear in the world we live in*
> *today. Never have there been more Christians, in more churches, in more*
> *nations, speaking more languages of the world. But I think it would also*

---

8 Landa Cope. *An Introduction to The Old Testament Template*. (Seattle, WA: YWAM Publishing, 2011).

9 Landa Cope. *An Introduction to The Old Testament Template*.

be fair to say that never has the spread of the church had less impact on surrounding communities. The Christian church today is a huge church and a weak church because we have lost most of the gospel message. We can say that the social, economic, and judicial issues of our communities are not our concern because we have a split view of the world. Spiritual leaders do need to concern themselves with secular matters.[10]

Wherever there is sickness, it needs to be healed, be it among races or in broken homes or in the community. The Church is called to cast out devils, and some of them are in the systems. We do not need to stop bringing the message of salvation, but we desperately need to discover God's way of dealing with the problems destroying the nation. When a few more of the ninety million professing Christians in America get this, the body of Christ will not only be large but multifaceted and will recover relevance and lost influence.

Meanwhile, families collapse, the poor suffer, police get vilified, courts become political, the economy is broken by debt and greed, and the world sees us branded in their mind as, "Republicans against gays and abortion" instead of the *vibrant counter culture that persuades.*

REFORMATION VERSUS REVIVAL

Where we are now is a defining moment. Reformation from the top down is what has to happen in order to see a historic change in nations. We must move into business, entertainment, and media to tell a different story. We need to advance into the colleges and universities where Marxists are currently educating our children. Remember, Jesus says in Matthew, "*Go therefore and make disciples of all the nations, baptizing them in the name of the Father and of the Son and of the Holy Spirit, teaching them to observe all things that I have commanded you.*"[11] **That cultural change comes from the top down and rarely, if ever, from the bottom up.**

True, there are incidents of political revolutions and economic revolts that occur from the bottom up, but they are almost always short-lived until they find allies at the gates of influence who champion the ideas. Martin

---

10 Landa Cope. *An Introduction to The Old Testament Template.*
11 Matthew 28:19-20 (NKJV).

Luther needed the German princes to support the Reformation. He told them, "The money of Germany is defying nature and flying over the Alps to Rome."[12] He was suggesting that the princes of Germany were behaving like puppets and painted a vivid picture of how the taxes collected by the Church in Germany were being used to fuel the inexhaustible corruption of the papacy at that time.

> REFORMATION IS INSTITUTIONAL AND REVIVAL IS INTERPERSONAL. UNLESS INSTITUTIONS ARE REFORMED, REVIVAL WILL HAVE LIMITED IMPACT.

He was saying, why are you paying a ten percent tithe to Rome when you could keep all that money? The princes knew if they embraced the ideas of Luther, they could take over the land previously owned by the church and grow even more powerful. The princes could also shut down the church's monasteries. In effect the princes could become more wealthy and powerful. They compared notes and could see Luther's movement had sufficient popularity, a strong "pattern of public persuasion" to enable them to break with Rome if they did so in unison. And that is what happened. The pattern of the house and the gatekeepers in government was repeated again. Luther the priest was in need of governors if he was to be protected and his movement expanded. Long-term cultural change always occurs from the top down. In other words, the work of permanent change is the work of gatekeeper elites. They provide legitimacy, creative direction, and management to the culture-shaping institutions in a society.

What about revival? Revival is for the church. It's important to understand that reformation is institutional and revival is interpersonal. Unless institutions are reformed, revival will have limited impact. Revival, which is what Christians are often looking for, works from the bottom up. That's why it's called a "grassroots" revival. When people become revived (awakened), they become reformers who work in the institutions to bring about transformation.

---

12 Chris LeClair. "Martin Luther: Wrecking Ball of Unintentional Reformation." DokuWiki. Creative Commons, March 14, 2012. https://dokuwiki.noctrl.edu/doku.php?id=ger%3A102%3A2012%3Awinter%3Achris_leclair_-_martin_luther.

ANARCHY AND EMPIRE

There is a reformation taking place in many nations as populist movements are raising up Cyrus-type leaders, pitting them against globalists who desire to create a world order that empowers their economic interests. This leads us back to the Chaos Code and the significance of the destiny of nations and the all-important emergence of Cyrus-type leaders like Donald Trump, Victor Orbán, Jair Bolsonaro, Boris Johnson, Andrzej Duda, and many others. We need to connect the dots. It is time for Christians in the West to develop a biblical worldview about God's plan for nations and the coming conflict, *not* with progressives, Democrats, or socialists, but with empire.

The liberal vision of pulling down borders and uniting mankind under one universal rule has been the ambition of man since the fall; the Egyptian Pharaohs, Babylonian kings, Roman emperors, the Roman Catholic Church after Constantine, Caliphates, Marxists, China, the EU elites, and American elites all possessed the ambition of empire. What empires do is offer peace to nation-states in exchange for their independence (including their ability to think and act as an independent nation). This is a *big* idea and the battle we are facing.

Think of a continuum from left to right with anarchy being on the extreme left and total dictatorship by a global elite on the right. The modern nation-state is the God-inspired idea that fits in the middle. Nobody wants anarchy. Government is a good thing; it restrains lawlessness and anarchy. The sinful nature of man needs government, but we want something between anarchy of pillaging bands of gangs and subordination to the "Gestapo" type of empire.

Yoram Hazony says:

Empire and anarchy are the horns of a dilemma that has dogged mankind's steps since antiquity. The earliest political images of the Bible—the story of the tower of Babylon, for example, in which the leadership about cities sought to unite humanity under one language in a single community of purpose; and that of Noah's Ark, a tiny, familiar community cast out of a violent and anarchic mankind—give a sense of how deeply these two evils impress themselves on the thought of our forefathers." And indeed, the problem of empire and anarchy is central to the political teaching of Hebrew scripture. What the prophets of Israel proposed in response to this dilemma was a third type of political order: the distinctive Israelite institution of the national state, which seeks to transcend the dilemma of empire and anarchy by retaining what is most vital in each, while discarding what makes each of them most dangerous.[13]

The God of Israel stepped into the space between anarchy and empire. The Bible introduces an entirely new political conception: a self-governing people with territorial boundaries, who were not prohibited from moving beyond the boundaries they had been given. This nation would not be ruled by foreigners from thrones in a far-off empire but, instead, by rulers drawn from the ranks of the nation itself, with the model of government being God over the people and the people over government. This model is seen in the New Testament where the apostles ran into a problem with managing the growing church and told their people, *"Brothers, select seven men who are well respected and are full of the Spirit and wisdom. We will give them this responsibility."*[14] Empire is the byproduct of man's pride attempting to do what only the Messiah Jesus can do. It is the promise of a utopia without Christ and will produce a counterfeit kingdom with a false Christ.

NATIONS WERE GOD'S IDEA

Nations were God's idea long before evangelism, soul winning, and healings. In the Old Testament, whenever God wanted to bless someone special, He would give them a child and a promise of nations.

The movement to create a one-world government, a world without walls, is in fact a world in defiance of God's boundaries. God put a boundary around Eden and limited access into the garden to one point. Wise parents will put a safe boundary around their children. When activists chant, "No border, no wall, no USA at all," they are chanting for the destruction of the nation. When speaking to Athens, Paul said, *"And he has made from one blood every nation of men to dwell on all the face of the earth, and has determined their preappointed times and boundaries of their dwellings."*[15]

---

13 Yoram Hazony. *The Virtue of Nationalism.* (New York: Basic Books, 2018).
14 Acts 6:3 (NLT).
15 Acts 17:26 (NKJV).

God Himself has given nations two things: first, a period of history to seek Him and hopefully find Him, and second, He gave them boundaries.

When Paul and Barnabas were speaking to the Greeks in Lystra, they spoke of nations, "*Turn from these useless things to the living God, who made the heaven, the earth, the sea, and all things that are in them, **who in bygone generations allowed all nations to walk in their own ways**.*"[16]

In generations past, God was only concerned with one nation, the nation of Israel; but after the resurrection of Christ, that changed. God is now calling all nations to respond to Christ. The Father is intent on delivering to His Son the promise in Psalm 2:8 (NKJV), "*Ask of Me, and I will give You the nations for Your inheritance, And the ends of the earth for Your possession.*"

SHEEP AND GOAT NATIONS

Matthew records exactly when Jesus will receive his inheritance: "*When the Son of Man comes in His glory, and all the holy angels with Him, then He will sit on the throne of His glory. **All the nations will be gathered before Him, and He will separate them one from another, as a shepherd divides his sheep from the goats.**"*[17]

The nations will be judged and separated into sheep or goats. What makes a nation a sheep or a goat nation? The verse continues:

*And He will set the sheep on His right hand, but the goats on the left. Then the King will say to those on His right hand, "Come, you blessed of My Father, inherit the kingdom prepared for you from the foundation of the world: for **I was hungry** and you gave Me food; **I was thirsty** and you gave Me drink; **I was a stranger** and you took Me in; **I was naked** and you clothed Me; **I was sick** and you visited Me; **I was in prison** and you came to Me." Then the righteous will answer Him, saying, "Lord, when did we see You hungry and feed You, or thirsty and give You drink? When did we see You a stranger and take You in, or naked and clothe You? Or when did we see You sick, or in prison, and come to You?" And the King*

---

16 Adapted from 1 Samuel 12:21.
17 Matthew 25:31–32 (NKJV).

*will answer and say to them, "Assuredly, I say to you, **inasmuch as you did it to one of the least of these My brethren, you did it to Me.**"*[18]

The defining issue between a sheep nation and goat nation will be, "*as much as you have **done to the least of these My brethren** you have done so to Me.*"[19] Nations will be judged on the basis of how they treat the brethren of Jesus.

Who then are the brethren? Fortunately the Bible answers this directly. Once while teaching, Jesus was interrupted by His mother. "*Someone told Him, 'Look, Your mother and brothers are standing outside, wanting to speak to you.' But Jesus replied, 'Who is My mother, and who are My brothers?' **Pointing to His disciples**, He said, 'Here are My mother and My brothers. For whoever does the will of My Father in heaven is My brother and sister and mother.'*" [20] Who are Jesus's brothers? From this verse we see it's His disciples!

When Jesus returns, He will sit on His throne and gather the nations. They will be separated based on how they responded to Jesus in the form of His people. He will return as the Hebrew Messiah, and the issue at the center of His judgment will be the treatment of the Christian and the Jewish people. This aligns with Bible teaching that prior to the return of Christ there will be a period of intense persecution for the people of God, and the way they treat His people is the way they treat Him. Jesus will deal with these nations personally upon His return.

Consider how Jesus identifies with His persecuted people when dealing with Saul of Tarsus. Saul was laying waste to the church, putting **many of the saints** in prison, forcing them to blaspheme, and condemning them to death. When Jesus confronted him, he fell to the ground and heard a voice saying, "*Saul, Saul, **why are you persecuting Me?***"[21] It is clear that when Saul was persecuting the body of Christ, he was persecuting Jesus. "*As much as you have done to the least of these my brethren you have done to Me.*"[22] Jesus identifies with His people.

---

18 Matthew 25:33–40 (NKJV).
19 Adapted from Matthew 25:40
20 Matthew 12:47–50 (Berean Study Bible).
21 Acts 26:14 (NLT).
22 Adapted from Matthew 25:40 (KJV).

A sheep nation is one that to some degree protects or keeps malicious forces from devouring the Christian and Jewish people. These sheep nations that have shown the people of God mercy wherever they have encountered His people in situations of need—whether hungry, thirsty, strangers, naked, sick, or imprisoned—will likewise be shown mercy. Conversely, the "goat" nations who have failed to show mercy will not be shown mercy.

These two types of nations are being formed right now; and as a result, this is the chapter of history we are locked in. Sheep nations are also the "S" in the Chaos code. They are the last step, because they are the ultimate goal we are after!

HEALTHY NATIONALISM

The creation of nations was God's idea. Nations, just like people, are unique. They have different shapes and sizes, but all are equally valuable. As God has given different gifts and callings to individuals, He has created nations with their own unique design and opportunities, be it in the geography or the people. Every nation has a redemptive gift wrapped up in its people. Redemptive gifts are in each nation. These attributes are recorded as motivational gifts in the book of Romans: exhorter, teacher, ruler, prophet, servant, mercy, and giver. The Philippines is a joyful servant nation. Canada is a mercy nation. Italy is an exhorter nation. Singapore is a teacher nation. America is a prophetic nation. The diagram below is from Arthur Burk, who has done quite a bit of teaching on the redemptive gifts of nations.

The Redemptive Gifts of Some Nations[23]

Sorted By Country:

Country	Gift	Country	Gift	Country	Gift
Afghanistan	Prophet	Ghana	Exhorter	Philippines	Giver
Argentina	Exhorter	Haiti	Prophet	Poland	Giver
Armenia	Giver	Hungary	Prophet	Portugal	Servant
Australia	Mercy	India	Servant	Romania	Giver
Austria	Mercy	Indonesia	Giver	Russia	Ruler
Barbados	Teacher	Iran	Ruler	Scotland	Prophet
Belgium	Teacher	Iraq	Prophet	Singapore	Teacher
Bolivia	Servant	Ireland	Teacher	South africa	Giver
Brazil	Giver	Israel	Giver	South korea	Giver
Cambodia	Giver	Italy	Exhorter	Spain	Prophet
Canada	Mercy	Japan	Giver	Sudan	Servant
China	Ruler	Jordan	Servant	Suriname	Servant
Costa rica	Teacher	Kenya	Giver	Sweden	Echorter
Cuba	Giver	Kurdistan	Teacher	Switzerland	Giver
Czech Republic	Prophet	Lebanon	Exhorter	Syria	Prophet
Denmark	Giver	Liechtenstein	Servant	Tanzania	Mercy
Egypt	Ruler	Mexico	Exhorter	Tibet	Teacher
El salvador	Servant	Mongolia	Prophet	Turkey	Prophet
England	Ruler	Nepal	Teacher	Uganda	Teacher
Eritrea	Prophet	Netherlands	Giver	United kingdom	Ruler
Ethiopia	Ruler	New Zealand	Prophet	United states	Prophet
Finland	Servant	Nigeria	Giver	Uruguay	Teacher
France	Exhorter	North korea	Giver	Vietnam	Servant
Germany	Prophet	Norway	Mercy	Wales	Exhorter
				Zambia	Servant

We see nations in the final chapter of the Bible operating as God desires, and each brings its glory into the city of God. The idea of the "glory of nations" is in stark contrast to the uniformity of nations that an empire establishes. The effort to create a global government without Christ will rob individuals of freedom and force nations into a structure that will inevitably fall into the orbit of the spirit of the antichrist.

As sheep nations pull back from the idea of global governance it is healthy nationalism that is feeding the growing patriotic devotion to one's shared geography, history, language, customs, and faith. What is nationalism though? The media likes to link "nationalism" to Nazis, but this is not what nationalism is at all.

---

23 Arthur Burke, "The Redemptive Gifts of Some Nations." Sapphire Leadership Group, 2017, http://theslg.com/img/cms/redemptivegiftspdf/Redemptive_Gifts_of_Nations_2015.pdf.

The first definition in Merriam-Webster for *nationalism* is "loyalty and devotion to a nation."[24] In a second paragraph, it adds, "especially: a sense of national consciousness exalting one nation above all others and placing primary emphasis on promotion of its culture and interests as opposed to those of other nations or supranational groups." The second definition shows how cultural conditioning works into language, because "loyalty and devotion" can exist for a country and not exist at the expense of another country. When the World Cup is on TV or when the Olympics are happening, we all turn into a nationalist rooting for our nation, not for a unified global team, but for *our* team, our nation, to win.

For nearly four hundred years, the principle of national independence served as the foundation for a better, freer world, but World War I and World War II changed everything. The world became traumatized by these catastrophic conflicts and became vulnerable to a new ceaselessly repeated narrative: that "nationalism caused two world wars and the Holocaust." But this is one of the great untruths of our time. The left tries to link Adolph Hitler with the idea of a "right winger," but right-wing conservatives actually want to limit the power of government. Hitler was in fact a socialist—a member of the nationalist socialist party. He was an imperialist. If his ambitions had been limited to ruling Germans, it would have been terrible for Germany; but the French, the British, the Russians, and everyone else would have been spared a world war. Sadly, European elites learned the wrong lesson from World War II, believing that independent nations are inherently dangerous. Better, they reasoned, that all countries should live under one government and let go of the patriotism that breeds conflict.

Christians sometimes struggle to balance patriotism with the principle of "loving your neighbor as yourself."[25] Is it possible to be thankful for the acts of God that have given you the blessing of your nation and reconcile this with a love for other people and respect for their nation? Of course. The principle of loving your neighbor as yourself can be applied to nations as well as to individuals. What we need to do is define the

24 *Merriam-Webster.com.* s.v. Nationalism, Def.1. Merriam-Webster, 2020.
25 Adapted from Matthew 19:19.

difference between "healthy nationalism" and "unhealthy nationalism." The best clarification about what unhealthy nationalism looks like comes from Dennis Prager:

> *Nationalism is evil when it celebrates race, but that is not nationalism; it is racism. Nationalism and racism may be conjoined, as German Nazism did. But they are not definitionally related. Some Americans have conjoined American nationalism with race… but American nationalism—based as it is on the motto "e pluribus unum" ("out of many, one")—by definition includes Americans of all races and ethnicities. That is how conservatives define American nationalism. I have never met a conservative who defined American national identity as definitionally "white."*[26]

This is the root behind the popular but erroneous understanding of nationalism you hear thrown around on MSNBC and CNN. It comes out of a one-sided analysis of World War II. Notice healthy nationalism was not celebrated when Winston Churchill and FDR used a positive call to national pride trumpeting the virtue of democracy in the face of Nazi tyranny.

Many on the left view American flag-loving conservatives and Bible believers as narrow minded, poorly educated, and racist. In their minds, clearly we don't know enough to manage our future, so they will do it for us. Liberals see Christians and patriots as bigoted nationalists, blind to our privilege and lacking in compassion and generosity. This is in spite of repeated findings that conservatives in the United States give a larger percentage of their money and time to charity than do liberals.

The quest to vilify nationalism explains why they tear down statues, burn the flag, burn the Bible, and dishonor the National Anthem. These middle-class values and symbols reinforce the nation's ability to define "American" citizenship. To them, America must come down, and preferably come down hard, so it can take its humbled and chastened seat in the new world order.

---

26 Dennis Prager. "Is Nationalism Bad?" JewishPress.com. https://www.jewishpress.com/indepth/columns/pragers-perspective/is-nationalism-bad/2019/06/27/.

THE ANATOMY OF POWER

While the Chaos Code explains that the shifting tectonic plates of our day involve the tension between nations versus empire, we should discuss how the narrative is manipulated to control the masses. While American Christians are focused on elections, the game is not about America; it is about world power. America—and Trump—must be moved out of the way for the power transfer to happen.

It is strange that there is not more thinking among Christians about the anatomy of power in culture. It is a subject that makes Christians feel awkward. So let's talk about what power really is. Max Weber, a German sociologist and political scientist (1864-1920), arrived at a simple definition of power: "the possibility of imposing one's will upon the behavior of another person's."[27] How does this definition apply to Christians? Jesus imposed His will on storms, sickness, demons, and death, yet did not impose His will on people.

Freedom is a form of power, or else dictators would not seek to remove it. Freedom is the individual's power to exist independent of the state. All such independence and autonomy are a threat. Economic control is easiest; what is harder is controlling people's thoughts and speech. For this reason the Christian religion is viewed adversarially by progressives, communists, Hindu nationalists and Islamic states. We should get familiar with the anatomy of power and how it shows up in society. There are three *instruments* of power:

- **Coercive power** has the ability to impose punishment. It wins submission by threat of pain and social consequence.

- **Compensatory power** wins support by the offer of reward. It works by promise of personal gain or benefit, approval, promotion, or prosperity.

- **Conditioned power** is the shaping of opinions, beliefs, conscience, convictions, and worldview. The earlier you start, the better.

---

27 Philo, Greg, and Paul Walton. "Max Weber On Self-Interest and Domination." *Social Theory and Practice 2*, no. 3 (1973). http://www.jstor.org/stable/23558893.

If the 7M world is not influenced by us, then these three instruments of power will shape the choices people make; the coercive power will be *fear,* the compensatory power will be *greed,* and the conditioned power will be *deception.*

On June 1, 2020, my friend Jeremiah Johnson predicted there were three dangerous waves that would hit the nation. The first wave would be fear, the second wave would be anger, and the third wave would be greed. Johnson says these three waves are designed to "disrupt systems, divert attention, and release chaos in the land."[28] Think about it, the China pandemic struck fear into hearts and shattered our economy, driving us into record debt and unemployment; that was wave one. Wave two was a flood of rampant anger originally sparked by the barbaric death of George Floyd but then taken over by professional street activists and anarchists who destroyed hundreds of minority-owned businesses, injured and killed law enforcement, and inaugurated a new Marxist wing of the Democratic party with enormous street appeal. Now we are about to see wave three hit America as the devil tries to do everything he can to lie, cheat, and steal this election so that he holds on to the remaining gates of influence he has. It amazes me how the three *instruments* of power closely resemble what Johnson says. I believe that all three waves will be intertwined with seducing force, so convincingly that even the elect of God, if possible, will be deceived.

ONE RING TO RULE THEM ALL

The battle over America is not just about America; it is about the destiny of nations in an era of increasing global governance. The United States under Donald Trump is a restraining force.

J.R. Tolkien's classic *Lord of the Rings* told a tale that revolved around the quest for power and control over the lives of others. Its themes speak to us today. A dark sorcerer named Sauron fashioned nineteen rings of power to disperse among the realms of men, elves, and dwarves. What he did not tell them is that he fashioned one ring for himself that would give

---

28 https://www.facebook.com/JeremiahJohnson.tv/posts/an-urgent-prophetic-alert-and-warning-released-on-june-1-2020dear-saints-and-lea/2582980608655962/

him power over all the others. Inscribed in the ring of power were words only visible when the ring was heated in the fire:

> One Ring to rule them all, One Ring to find them,
> One Ring to bring them all and in the darkness bind them.[29]

The central character in Tolkien's tale is not from the realm of men, elves, or dwarves. In his story, the unsuspecting hero is a hobbit. These endearing characters were small of stature, congenial, and seldom adventured out from their shires. Though hospitable, they were suspicious of outsiders. What made them indispensable in the destruction of the ring was their resistance to the ring's seductive power. It had its effect, but Hobbits were more resistant, probably because they were less ambitious in worldly affairs.

I cannot help but say how often I think of my generation in the West as being a bit like Tolkien's hobbits. Certainly not like the pioneers of the book of Acts, or the courageous saints in Nigeria in the face of Boko Haram, or the underground church in China, Iran, or Nigeria. When it comes to the hobbit comparison, I am thinking of the rank-and-file believer in Western society today. Most of us would prefer to live out our lives undisturbed and not bother others. We have our spiritual pursuits but stay mostly inside the "shire" unless we venture off on a mission trip. We love to fellowship, sing, and tell stories of some exaggerated exploit or some friend's adventure. We are, for the most part, an unsuspecting, trusting company that may fall prey to gossip and idleness but are seldom at the center of grand affairs and worldly intrigues.

Not so the children of this age. They have plans, schemes, and ambitions to conquer the world. In America, the ambitious leftists can almost taste it. They have every ring but one—the ring of ultimate power. They came so close but were "robbed" of it in 2016. They have manifested like denizens of hell ever since. They must have this ring to complete their conquest, and it is on the hand of Donald Trump. They must have Trump's executive office. The lure of the ring speaks to both sides of the

---

29 J.R.R. Tolkien, *The Lord of the Rings* (New York: Del Rey/Ballantine Books, 2012).

aisle. Democrats want the power, and Washington Republicans want to return to the status quo.

The role Donald Trump seeks for America is that of an independent nation, supporting a global community of independent nations. The election looks increasingly like it will not be decided on November 3, as some rogue states are counting mail-in ballots as long as they are postmarked by midnight on election night. This means it could be a Trump landslide on election day, and then—surprise, surprise—ballots begin to arrive, postmarked November 3, 2020, with time stamps of 9:00 p.m., 10:00 p.m., or even 11:59 p.m. We could see within days that landslides turn into a margin, and then potentially a Trump defeat. That scenario doesn't even include the normal illegal ballots, ballet harvesting, and voting irregularities. The key indicator is going to be major networks like FOX, AP, and even Facebook not declaring a winner on election night. If that doesn't happen, the election results will be contested, and the debate could last not just weeks but months. This uncertainty will unleash the street units of the Democrat party—Antifa, BLM, and 100 other funded operations—into open assault on America. It may be that the Supreme Court will end up appointing Trump as president during a period of unparalleled national chaos. This Trump victory won't stop the insanity; it will only serve to escalate the distress all the more.

We live in a rare moment of world history. The post-COVID global economic reset will require an economically sound America. This global order must not shift toward China. The window is open for a short period of time for Donald Trump, with his unique economic qualifications and Cyrus qualities, to establish and solidify an alliance of democratic nation-states, based upon shared values, a respect for the rule of law, and the retaining of sovereign boundaries. He is the one person who can secure that global order because he's a negotiator and a leader and he has the energy and brainpower to understand world economics.

This election is not about the US; it's about the world. You know who is watching this election? The oppressed in Tehran and in the streets of Beirut, trying to throw off Hezbollah. The terrorized Christians in Hong Kong are watching. They face new laws under Chinese occupation under which government forces can drag them off to the mainland where they can be disciplined, placed in slave labor, or exterminated and forgotten. Nervous Christians in Taiwan are watching as President Xi Jinping has warned them that their assimilation will be done by either peaceful surrender or armed conflict. The voters in Taipei are watching. They threw out the Chinese Communist Party with a landslide, waving American flags and carrying posters of Donald Trump dressed like a superhero. The people watching us include nearly twenty leaders in various levels of government whom I've talked to in South America who fear the same Marxist insurgency hitting America is rising to overturn their democracies and religious freedom as well.

This is the scenario we face in the 2020 election, and the endgame is the destiny of nations. The Chaos Code lays out the nature of the opposition we face. God will have sheep nations or the devil will have an empire. The election in America, and elections around the world are not about political parties, "Republican versus Democrat," or "capitalism versus socialism." It has always been, and will always be, sheep nations versus the empire ambitions of a one-world government. The labels we place on the political—policy, party, and ideology—are tools used to either strengthen sheep nations or weaken them. This is the cycle we see repeated throughout history, in the Chaos Code, and what will continue to happen until Christ returns.

CHAPTER 5

THE BILLY GRAHAM PROPHECY

"If we fail to solve this moral and spiritual crisis we may be doomed like the great nations of the past."
— *Billy Graham*

The truth is, *no* Israelite should have remained in Persia after the decree of Cyrus. Yet only a small remnant of 49,000 answered the call to travel with Zerubbabel back to Jerusalem. The majority stayed in Babylon. They had built their lives in Babylon, raised children there, and invested in the prosperity of the new location. In this sense, they were doing what Jeremiah admonished them to do: *"Also, seek the peace and prosperity of the city to which I have carried you into exile. Pray to the LORD for it, because if it prospers, you too will prosper."*[1] To them, this was the new home. It was an understandable, though selfish inclination. On one hand, the children of Abraham must fight for the boundaries of the inheritance God has allotted; yet on the other, they must be ever seeking a city whose builder and maker is God. In this way, we contend for Christ's inheritance on the earth while confessing like Peter that we are pilgrims, passing through this momentary struggle. They had the security of Cyrus's domain where they could continue to build the wealth they had accrued. Staying, however, would almost cost them their lives.

---

1 Jeremiah 29:7

After the remnant left with Zerubbabel, there would now be two groups God was going to speak to—those who went back to Jerusalem and those who stayed in Babylon:

- The ones who left the security of Persia for a desolate Judea **would hear His** prophets **and** see His acts.

- The ones who stayed in Persia **would not hear** Him speak, but they would see Him act.

The story of what happened to the Jews who chose to remain in Babylon is the story of Esther. It is a book about God's covert works. This is a book about a nation in crisis that ties directly into the Cyrus Code found in Haggai, Zechariah, Ezra, and Nehemiah! While one part of the Jewish family moved rubble and dealt with the threat of rival tribes in Jerusalem, the Hebrew citizens of Persia faced a more sinister political faction that sought to kill them and take their property. The scope of this genocide would have been larger than Hitler's Holocaust.

ESTHER

The hope of Jewish survival would arise from a most unlikely source. It would not be weapons and men of war that God would use as His instrument of deliverance—instead, it would be a young woman. Her name was Esther. She became queen because her predecessor, Queen Vashti (meaning "beautiful woman"), offended her husband, the Persian King Ahasuerus. Worse yet, she embarrassed him in front of his subjects in the middle of a banquet. The king wanted her to put on the royal crown and display her beauty before his guests, but she refused. It was this act of defiance that caused her to be removed as queen. Not long after, a nationwide search began for her royal replacement, and it was Esther who was crowned queen. We do not know what happened to her parents; but we know she was an orphan, adopted by her older cousin Mordecai, who raised her as his own.

The book of Esther is more than a Cinderella story; in the midst of it all was a providential hand at work elevating Esther to her new position. Chaos was about to erupt in the land, wrought by an evil man named Haman, and Esther would be the one to stop him. Haman emerged from out of nowhere and rose quickly to a place of influence in the king's court, becoming a senior political advisor to the king. He was a man held in high esteem—so high, in fact, that the king gave Haman a special seat of honor above all the other nobles. Every royal official at the king's gate was required to kneel before Haman when he passed. All of them did kneel, except one. The one man who refused was none other than Esther's cousin, Mordecai. Haman became so offended that he wanted to kill Mordecai **and** all of Mordecai's people, the Jews.[2]

He craftily prepared legislation that would isolate and target the Hebrew people on the basis of their faith practices, claiming that they had customs that were different from others and were a threat to the king's interests. He built into his scheme an incentive plan allowing anyone who participated in killing the Jews to take possession of their wealth and private property.

To accomplish this plan, Haman required the consent of the king. He offered to pay 345 metric tons of silver to the king's treasury in exchange for his approval, knowing he would extract a substantial amount from the plundered wealth and property of the Jews. This figure was two-thirds of the annual budget of the Persian empire—a huge sum! Haman estimated that he could pay the king and still make a massive profit. *"Keep the money and do with the people as you please,"*[3] the king replied. In heartless disregard for the lives of his subjects, King Ahasuerus handed Haman his signet ring so the decree could be made official. It was a large ring bearing the image of the royal house. Once the ring made an imprint on the wax seal of a document, the matter was legally binding and paid for. Once the wax hardened, the matter could not be undone.

With the plan approved, Haman began to build gallows to hang Mordecai and his family from. He then consulted occult astrologists, who cast lots to choose the timing for the attack. They wanted the gods of Persia to select the exact day to commence their massacre and plunder the wealth of the Jews. The lot fell upon the thirteenth day of the twelfth month.

Haman was being driven by an ancient spirit whose motivation was, and still is, to annihilate the children of God. The Jews were not dealing with a human agenda; it was witchcraft at the highest level of political

---

2 Adapted from Esther 3:5.

3 Adapted from Esther 3:11

conspiracy. This spirit was the same one in Daniel's writings that resisted Gabriel for twenty-one days—it was the "prince of Persia." No doubt, this was the power at work behind Haman's plot and his casting of lots. It is a spirit that politicizes every aspect of life. Sound familiar? How many athletes have been forced to take a knee who simply want to play ball?

When the decree for the destruction of the Jews was made public, Mordecai went through the city wailing loudly and bitterly. He took his cry right up to the king's gate. When Esther heard of his display, she sent a member of the court to find out what had happened. Mordecai sent word back to Esther regarding the edict, telling her she needed to personally petition the king and beg for mercy for her people.

However, to do so, she would have to initiate contact with the king, which was dangerous because nobody, male or female, could approach the inner court without an invitation from the king. Uninvited intruders to the king's court faced a sentence of death unless the king chose to extend his golden scepter in their direction. Esther had not been summoned in thirty days.

Mordecai understood the risk, but he warned her that she should not think that she or her family were safe or would survive the purge just because she was living in the king's house. In fact, he assured her the opposite, saying that if she did nothing, both Esther and her family would perish and that God would raise up deliverance from another quarter. He gave purpose to her entire journey by saying, *"Who knows but that you were brought to the kingdom for such a time as this?"*[4]

Esther knew this was a potential suicide mission, but she accepted the assignment, saying, *"If I perish, I perish."*[5] Esther understood she would be absolutely dependent upon God for her survival, so she requested that all Jews who could be reached engage in a fast, neither eating nor drinking for the next three days.

After the three-day fast, Esther approached the king; and when he saw her, she obtained favor. The king extended his golden scepter toward her, dictating she could come near. She did not immediately make her plea; instead, she asked for the pleasure of the king's company. She requested that the king, along with his exalted friend Haman, join her for dinner.

---

4 Esther 4:14 (NKJV)
5 Esther 4:16 (NIV)

He agreed. That evening, after a night of food and wine, the king asked her what she had on her heart to talk to him about. She sensed the timing was not yet right to make her petition and instead requested a *second* dinner. The next evening, the king again asked what was on Esther's mind. At that, she fell to her knees and pleaded for her life and the life of her people. King Ahasuerus was indignant that his wife was in threat of losing her life and demanded to know who was threatening her, at which point she turned and pointed toward the man who planned their destruction: *"It's this wicked Haman."*[6] Immediately, the king connected that this was the edict he had issued with his own signet ring. He rose from the table in anger and departed to walk in the queen's garden, adjacent to where they dined. Haman, knowing the king's notorious temper, rose to plead with Esther; but in doing so, he stumbled upon her couch—at the very moment the king returned. Ahasuerus burst out, *"What! Will you sexually assault the queen also right here in my presence?"*[7] Immediately, Haman was hung from the gallows he had erected the day before to hang Mordecai from.

The king could not cancel Haman's decree, but instead told Esther, *"Write another decree in the king's name on behalf of the Jews as seems best to you, and seal it with the king's signet ring."* In Scripture, the signet ring was a highly symbolic artifact that spoke of God's royal authorization. Esther and Mordecai made an official decree to the Jews, to get them ready to defend their lives and overcome their enemies. They wrote to the Jews who were in every city to *"gather and defend their lives; to destroy, to slay, and to wipe out any armed force that might attack them, their little ones, and women; and to take their enemies' goods for spoil."*[8]

Scripture records the exact day on which Esther and Mordecai were authorized to reverse Haman's curse: *"the month of Sivan, on the twenty-third day,"*[9] which was exactly seventy days after Haman wrote the edict to annihilate the Jews.[10] Have you noticed the number seventy keeps coming

---

6 Esther 7:6 (ISV)

7 See Esther 7:8.

8 Adapted from Esther 8:11 (Everyday Life Bible).

9 Esther 8:9 (ESV)

10 See Jason A. Smith. "Esther 8–10." https://sermons.faithlife.com/sermons/221672-esther-8-10

up in the code? In Scripture, numbers always mean something. In this instance, the number is symbolic of the seventy years the Jews were held in Babylonian captivity. The devil had no intention of letting the Jews leave.

With a new edict released, the Jews had enough time to prepare for the attack. This is important: **the attack was never canceled, but the Jews, being forewarned, were able to prepare and mobilize and deal with it**. The Bible says, *"On the day the enemies of the Jews had hoped to overpower them, the opposite occurred, in that the Jews overpowered those who hated them."*[11] The Jews, however, were under strict instructions by Mordecai not to touch their enemies' possessions. In striking contrast to their foes, the Jews were to act for their survival and not for plunder. Now, rather than being hunted, there was new prestige for the Jewish people in the courts of Persia as word got out that the queen was a Hebrew and that the king had installed Mordecai as the new prime minister.

The story of Esther was nearly rejected by scholars when they were assembling the books of the Bible—not because of its content, but because it never actually mentions the name of God directly. Instead, God's providential hand is hidden in the pages of Esther. For instance, God's name, though hidden, does appear in the book of Esther, concealed in acrostics—no less than eight times. The words "The Almighty," "Messiah," "I AM," "Yahweh," and "Yeshua" can be found in the text. In Esther, each of these eight hidden messages follows the story. Where God was reversing a development, the name was spelled backward; and where God was initiating an event, the name was spelled forward. The most interesting acrostic is found in Esther 3:11-12. Starting with the first letter in verse 11, and counting every sixth letter ten times, you discover the Hebrew phrase, *haman v'satan ray'yach*, which is translated "Haman and Satan stink." No kidding!

The fact that God did not want His name mentioned overtly in Esther contains a revelation. Even the name "Esther" means "something hidden." The Bible says, "It is the glory of God to conceal a matter and the glory of kings to search it out." God hides things so we will search for them, because once we discover them, they have increased value. The book of Esther is our final piece of the Chaos Code. To this day, the Jewish people celebrate Purim and remember that freedom is something that must be

---

11 Esther 9:1 (Everyday Life Bible).

defended. All nations will face their own Mordecai moments whenever a law, or another person's "sacred," requires that God's people bow down and violate their conscience.

NATIONS IN THE VALLEY OF DECISION

Since their inception, the Israelites have had to fight for their right to exist. Century after century, they have had to overcome the ancient spirit bent on their destruction. The *right* of Israel to exist is the central issue of the story of Purim and the books surrounding the Chaos Code. It is the central defining issue that confronts all nations during the period the code sets forth. This is clearly seen in Joel: ***"In those days and at that time when I restore the fortunes of Judah and Jerusalem I will gather all nations and bring them down to the Valley of Jehoshaphat."***[12]

Here, the prophet sets forth two perspectives as to how God deals with nations at the close of this age. One perspective shows mercy and restoration for Israel, but the other, judgment for all those nations who oppose and oppress Israel, claiming jurisdiction over Israel's land. The place ordained for judgment is called "the Valley of Jehoshaphat." The name "Jehoshaphat" means "the Lord judges." This is an actual location in Israel.

Joel continues:

Let the nations be roused; let them advance into the Valley of Jehoshaphat, for there I will sit to judge all the nations on every side.[13]

Multitudes, multitudes in the valley of decision! For the day of the Lord is near in the valley of decision.[14]

The prophet shows us that "the valley of the Lord's judgment" is also "the valley of decision." Every nation will face a Mordecai moment. Did they bow to the ancient evil spirit making war against God's people or stand to defend them? I believe nations are already being forced to make

---

12 Joel 3:1-2 (NIV).
13 Joel 3:12 (NIV)
14 Joel 3:14 (NIV)

decisions and are being weighed in the balance. The "valley of decision" depicts a place that God compels all nations to enter. Once they enter, they will not be able to exit until they have made a decision—a decision that determines the future of nations. This will be the only way out.

Two historic events have transpired since WWII that suggest the preconditions are in place for this moment of decision to take place. First, Israel's establishment as a nation-state in 1948 and second, it's retaking of Jerusalem in 1967. These events officially launched a last day's time clock. Cyrus-Trump's decision to move the US embassy to Jerusalem provoked a first round of emerging sheep and goat nations to go public and make their approval and disapproval of Jerusalem as the capital of Israel a matter of record. It was also an awkward moment for those nations who abstained from voting.

Many Scriptures reveal that, at the close of this age, God will judge nations on the basis of their attitude toward His people, the regathering of Israel, the restoration of their land, and the city of Jerusalem. The Messiah, His kingdom, His people, and Israel are a "stone of stumbling" for whoever picks it up the wrong way.

The decision required of nations will be clear. They must either submit to God's Word or reject it. Submission will entail aligning themselves with God's covenant purposes for Israel. Opposing God's covenant purposes for Israel will solidify rejection of His Word and will inevitably result in the judgment of nations, as forewarned. This is the code behind the shaking prophesied by Haggai that will rattle the heavens, the earth, and the nations. We are living through the fulfillment of the Chaos Code as Bible prophecy unfolds before our eyes. In the same way there is a regathering of Israel, there is a gathering of God's people in the nations of the earth. The rebuilding of the house is a real project. This coming harvest will be ushered in by people like you. Among you are the Esthers, Mordecais, Haggais, Zerubbabels, Nehemiahs, Ezras, and a very special company of people I call the **Statesmen Evangelists**.

THE BILLY GRAHAM PROPHECY

On February 21, 2018, one of the most influential embodiments of a Statesman Evangelist—the Reverend Billy Graham— went home to heaven. Seven days after his death, his humble pine plywood casket, built by inmates from Louisiana State Penitentiary, was taken to the US Capitol Rotunda in

Washington, DC, where leaders of nations came to pay their respects. Like in the book of Esther, God's message was hidden in plain sight. There was a massive prophetic transaction happening before our eyes. Most people missed it, but a transition occurred over America. To fully understand what God was doing, we need to first understand who Billy Graham was and the different ways God used him throughout the course of his life.

In 1934, a group of Charlotte businessmen used a portion of a family's dairy farm to gather for a day of prayer. On that day, the men prayed for the city of Charlotte, North Carolina, and asked that the Lord would raise up someone from their city to preach the gospel to the ends of the earth. Just a few months later, that prayer would be answered when the fifteen-year-old boy who lived on the very farm accepted Jesus Christ as Lord and Savior. It was a little-known evangelist named Mordecai Hamm who had the privilege of leading a young Billy Graham in a salvation prayer that would change the world forever.

Starting from a small Bible school in Florida, Graham soon found himself leading a historic revival in 1949 in Los Angeles, California. There, media baron William Randolph Hearst, a staunch anti-communist, received a random call from a Graham prayer warrior, telling him about the young evangelist's work. Hearst put out the message "Puff Graham" to his papers, and by mid-October, he had made Graham a front-page story. Other papers and magazines caught on, and a media circus followed. Graham's meetings swelled to a national revival of Christianity, impacting 100,000 people in a single day at Yankee Stadium and building up to more than two million people at Madison Square Garden over a sixteen-week-period in 1957.

During those years, Graham's message captured the nation's mood. Here was a young man seized with an apocalyptic vision of the West, specifically the United States, being swallowed up and destroyed by the devil, working through atheistic political forces. He was on fire with a message that gave meaning and context to the wave of panic that was felt in the nation. Among Graham's most enduring legacies from that time was his role in merging patriotism and Christianity in the public sphere—an arc that began during the Cold War. Billy linked democracy with religious freedom and set it against militant agnosticism embodied in the global ambitions of communism. His message was aimed at nothing less than national repentance and the survival of America. He believed that Americans enjoyed a period of history as a world super-power with unprecedented economic growth and freedom because Almighty God had blessed America with a responsibility in the world.

Graham further shaped the Cold War alignment of faith and the nation by personally recruiting Dwight Eisenhower to run for president in 1952. He offered advice at Eisenhower's campaign headquarters and helped select Scriptures for Ike to deliver in his stump speeches. All that work culminated in Graham's participating in Eisenhower's inauguration. The popular evangelist served as a constant source of support for the president. Graham and Eisenhower worked together over the next eight years, merging the message of godliness and patriotism. One of the biggest statesman contributions Graham made was forming the DC national prayer breakfast for both American parties and world leaders in 1953, an event that continues with global impact to this day. From Eisenhower's administration onward, Graham became a trusted confidant of American presidents and a familiar guest at the White House.

Graham's call took him into a global political environment as a statesman for Christ. He continued to adapt and focus his salvation message as he reached broader and more diverse audiences. He preached in London, Tokyo, Seoul, Bogota, Moscow, New Delhi, Saigon, Johannesburg, and scores of other nations, with more than 200 million people attending his events in person and countless others through television and radio. World leaders also understood the power Graham had as a source of political-social capital. Some nations viewed him as something they could use for propaganda purposes. The Soviets in 1982 thought they had scored a major coup by persuading Graham to attend a "peace" propaganda conference. The conference was called the "World Conference of Religious Workers for Saving the Sacred Gift of Life from Nuclear Catastrophe." The communists wanted to use the optics of Reverend Graham's visit to convey the idea that they were "open societies." Graham understood what they were doing, but he allowed himself to be used in this manner since it meant he could preach the gospel.

As the statesman aged, he stopped speaking to crowds but continued his long-established ministry of standing in the gap as a prayer intercessor for America. He continued to pray daily for America until his ninety-nine-year-old mortal body surrendered itself back to the One who gave him life. As Billy Graham faded from view, the collective memory of America as a

Christian nation likewise faded. What remained on that day, February 18, 2018, was the symbol of America's praying patriarch, whose body was at rest in the nation's Capitol. As the elder statesman ascended to his reward, I believe something new came down from heaven.

When the Old Testament prophet Elijah was taken up from earth into heaven in a chariot wrapped in fire, his young apprentice, Elisha, cried out after him, *"My Father, my Father, the chariots of Israel and the horseman thereof!"*[15] In Hebrew culture, the chariot and horsemen are a reference to God's protection over Israel. As young Elisha saw his prophetic father departing with chariots of Israel, he cried out as if to say, *"My father! What will become of Israel? What will become of me?"* His cry was the realization that the father's covering, **the covering for the nation, was departing!** It was indeed departing, but as Elijah went up in the chariot, something came down. Elijah's mantle descended to the earth so Elisha could pick it up. The mantle of intercession and prophetic ministry for Israel and its kings had passed to a new generation, and Elisha now had it! Elisha became the prophet who covered his nation.

All this applies to Billy Graham, the patriarch who prayed for America every day. As he went up, his mantle descended. President Trump presided over the transaction as he stood up at the memorial service in the US Capitol Rotunda and prayed, "Like the faithful of Charlotte once did, today we say a prayer for our country that **all across this land the Lord will raise up men and women like Billy Graham** to spread a message of love and hope to every precious child of God."[16]

Was the God who hides Himself unfolding a prophetic sign before the eyes of the nation? What we saw on the surface was the end of an era. Gone was the hour when evangelicals, like the Jews in Persia, could relax in the quiet security of their neighborhoods. Their faith was now an issue. Gone was the hour when Christian patriotism was the celebrated belief of

---

15 2 Kings 2:12 (KJV).

16 Donald Trump, "Remarks by President Trump at Ceremony Preceding the Lying in Honor of the Reverend Billy Graham" WhiteHouse Gov, 28 Feb 2018. https://www.whitehouse.gov/briefings-statements/remarkspresident-trump-ceremony-preceding-lying-honor-reverend-billy-graham/

the nation. The atmosphere was changing, but the mantle that fell would be like Elisha's mantle: a double portion of power for the hour at hand.

God chose the Feast of Purim in 2018 to mark Billy Graham's passing. It was a conspicuous boundary marker on display for the nation to see. My good friend Kim Clement predicted this boundary event. Kim had the unique ability to perceive things that would come to pass years in the future. He predicted, "Trump shall be a Trumpet."[17] As I recalled Trump's prayer for a new generation of Billy Grahams, I remembered that Kim also predicted that, after Reverend Graham's death, God would raise up two like him:

The Spirit of God says, even **as Billy Graham dies, I will raise up two of him**. *I will raise up two of "Billy Graham," says the Lord. God said, your soil surrendered him to Me, and so shall your soil receive him. For the Spirit of God says, I will raise up two great men, no—***one man and one woman**, *again from this soil. And God said, evangelism shall take place through the news media and the arts and in the business arena… In the day that he dies, the eyes of the prophets shall see the Lord high and lifted up.* **The prophetic shall gain a new dimension of sight…** *a* **dimension of sight that the Body of Christ has never seen.** *Do not say, 'but is he this denomination and that?' God said, two shall be raised up who shall become two nations and forces, and those that shall come from the world shall thank you.*

To hear a more detailed account of what Kim Clement said and what he foresaw for America, visit with me and Donnè Clement, his daughter, as we explore these remarkable predictions. Visit GodsChaosCode.com/Kim.

THE RISE OF STATESMEN EVANGELISTS

God has raised up voices like Graham's throughout history. Jan Hus (1369–1415) shaped Prague. John Knox (1514–1572) jolted Scotland. Abraham Kuyper (1837–1920) stormed the Netherlands. Myles Monroe (1954–2014) shaped the Bahamas. Pope John Paul II (1920–2005) freed Poland from

---

17 Kim Clement,"Trump Shall Become a Trumpet." YouTube. https://www.youtube.com/watch?v=r6niv0FN6iE.

Soviet agnosticism and, with that, contributed to the liberation of Eastern Europe. Martin Luther King, Jr. (1929-1968) brought justice and healing through peace as a Statesman Evangelist for civil rights. These preaching reformers taught, persuaded, and at times, thundered a message that forged a national identity that impacted the trajectory and destiny of the nations assigned to them. I call these individuals "Statesmen Evangelists."

They possess the unique ability to walk in the company of kings without compromising their message. While this subject is just opening up to many observers, there seem to be four common attributes of the Statesmen Evangelists:

1. **They Speak to the Destiny of Nations:** They have a world vision, yet they operate in their unique sphere of authority and influence in nations assigned to them. They infuse national identity, calling, and purpose into their listeners.

2. **They Deliver an Uncompromised Message:** They call their followers to radical biblical morality and spiritual awakening.

3. **They Issue a Spiritual Summons:** There is a tone of urgency and consequence in their message. They believe that rulers and nations are accountable to God, as He holds their times in His hands. They look at culture as something being "weighed in the balances" by God.

4. **They Are Called to Minister to Kings**: They have access into the lives of leaders and influencers. Like Samuel to King Saul and King David, they speak to the personal call of leaders. It is lonely at the top, and rulers need the friendship and confidentiality of a God-given friend. The Statesman Evangelist will pray for them and speak what the Lord tells them.

Now, more than ever, we need Statesmen Evangelists to preach the gospel, build unity in the nation, and keep reverence for Almighty God alive. A new generation of Christian preachers is about to emerge. God is even using the current condition of our nation to stir in them a sorrow for what is being taken and a righteous zeal to recover what is lost. Their message of repentance, the call back to God, and a return to true righteousness will be made clear. Just as Billy Graham was anointed by God to align the nation with its true identity rooted in Christ, these evangelists will be instrumental in calling the nation out of chaos and into its right mind, exalting Christ. The gospel will go forth with the same anointing, clarity, and power that attended Billy Graham's emergence on the national stage in 1948, warning America of the dangerous rise of militant agnosticism that threatens to destroy it if it does not repent. These ministries are the tip of the spear piercing the veil of deception wrapped over the American mind. A great harvest of souls will come out from under a spell as America enters its Third Great Awakening. I believe this awakening is connected to a spiritually seismic event that went largely unnoticed as it occurred in Washington, DC, on February 28, 2018, on the exact dates of the Feast of Purim.

WE WANT GOD!

I want to highlight one often overlooked exploit of a Statesman Evangelist, Pope John Paul II, as he took his place in history, freeing Poland from the clutches of atheistic communism. In 1978, Pope John Paul II, the newly appointed leader of the Catholic Church, desired to travel to his home country, Poland, to celebrate the 1,000th anniversary of the introduction of Christianity into Poland. His nation had been assimilated into the Soviet Union in 1945, at the close of World War II, as Poland fell under communist control and Europe was split in two. Europe was divided into the East—communist police states controlled by the Soviet Union and run by local communist parties and secret police—and the West—the democracies. During that time, the Communist Party launched the "The Polish Anti-Religious Campaign" in Poland, which, under the doctrine of Marxism, actively advocated for the disenfranchisement of religion and the promotion of atheism. The same regime conducted anti-religious propaganda throughout the school system as persecution raged against clergymen and monasteries. Religion was not outlawed outright, but the state was intent on converting the nation into an atheistic society.

The pope's desire to visit Poland was an obvious problem for the communists. If they refused the pope in his own country, they would appear to be insecure. Yet if they let him in, the people might begin to rise up against the communists, which could trigger a military confrontation. Ultimately, they decided to invite Pope John Paul, because the risk of looking weak would be too great an embarrassment. That decision would be the beginning of the toppling of the communist regimes in Europe.

When Pope John Paul II arrived on June 2, 1979, he knelt and kissed the ground of the worn gray tarmac at the airport outside Warsaw. As news of his appearance spread, the once-silent churches of Poland began to ring their bells. Masses of people lined the roads leading to Warsaw, where the pope was about to speak in the old city—all of them cheering and throwing flowers, applauding, and singing.

A million people stood in Victory Square as the pope arrived for Mass. Communist officials peered down on the crowd from windows of government buildings as he began to speak: "Together with you, I wish to sing a hymn of praise to Divine Providence, which enables me to be here as a pilgrim."[18] God's providential hand had raised up a Polish pope for such a time as this, to help deliver the Polish people from their long night of atheistic oppression.

Pope John Paul II, realizing the weight of the moment, continued:

> I must nonetheless with all of you ask myself why, precisely in 1978, after so many centuries of a well-established tradition in this field, a son of the Polish Nation, of the land of Poland, was called to the chair of Saint Peter. Christ demanded of Peter and the other apostles that they should be his "witnesses in Jerusalem and in all Judea and Samaria and to the end of the earth." Have we not the right, with reference to these words of Christ, to think that Poland has become nowadays the land of a particularly responsible witness?
>
> To think that one must come to this very place, to this land, on this route, to read again the witness of his Cross and his Resurrection? But if we accept all that I have dared to affirm in this moment, how many great duties and obligations arise? Are we capable of them?[19]

To preach Christ again in this place in which he had grown up, in a nation where most of the citizens were Catholic, under Communist rule,

---

18 John Paul II, "Holy Mass." https://www3.nd.edu/~amcadams/
Communism_2010/PopeinPoland.html

19 John Paul II, "Holy Mass." https://www3.nd.edu/~amcadams/
Communism_2010/PopeinPoland.html

was an act that required a bold Statesman Evangelist. It is hard to appreciate how much personal courage these statesmen must summon.

He reminded the crowd that Christ's commission was that we preach the gospel to the ends of the earth and that no matter what the government said, Christ's command was that the gospel be preached. He asked, essentially, "If we accept all that," then what is our duty and obligation as a witness for Christ? And in light of where they were, behind the iron curtain, was Poland ready to be that *particularly responsible witness?*

The pope had originally requested to hold Mass on a date commemorating an early martyr of the Church, but the Soviet government did not want to give him a date so pregnant with historic significance. Instead, they chose another date, which happened to be the day of Pentecost! Pentecost is the day the church celebrates the outpouring of the Holy Spirit in the upper room. After Christ had been raised from the dead, He promised that He would not leave us orphaned in the world, but would send to us the same mighty power that anointed Him. The Holy Spirit would soon dwell in His people. Just before His ascension, Jesus instructed His disciples to wait in Jerusalem until they were visited with *"power from on high."*[20] The Holy Spirit arrived as *"the sound of a rushing mighty wind,"*[21] filling the 120 gathered in the upper room and disbursing tongues of fire over their heads. They spoke out loud the *"wonderful works of God."*[22] Note carefully that they were not speaking in their own native languages; they were speaking in foreign tongues, the languages of other nations, which they had never spoken before! At that moment, they went out into the street, and Acts 2:5–11 records what happened next:

> *Now there were dwelling in Jerusalem God-fearing Jews from every nation under heaven. And when this sound rang out, a crowd came together in bewilderment, because each one heard them speaking his own language.*
>
> *Astounded and amazed, they asked, "Are not all these men who are speaking Galileans? How is it then that each of us hears them in*

---

20 Acts 1:8 (KJV)

21 Adapted from Acts 2:2

22 "Acts 2 Commentary." *Precept Austin,* 01 June 2019, https://www.preceptaustin. org/acts-2-commentary.

his own native language? Parthians, Medes, and Elamites; residents of Mesopotamia, Judea and Cappadocia, Pontus and Asia, Phrygia and Pamphylia, Egypt and the parts of Libya near Cyrene; visitors from Rome, both Jews and converts to Judaism; Cretans and Arabs—we hear them declaring the wonders of God in our own tongues!"[23]

It's in this unique story that the pope began to make the case that the salvation of man and the salvation of nations are intrinsically linked, and both belong to God. The pope said:

On the day of Pentecost there were gathered, in the Apostles and around them, not only the representatives of the peoples and tongues listed in the book of the Acts of the Apostles. Even then there were gathered about them the various peoples and nations that, through the light of the gospel and the power of the Holy Spirit, were to enter the Church at different periods and centuries. The day of Pentecost is the birthday of the faith and of the Church in our land of Poland also. It is the proclamation of the mighty works of God in our Polish language also. It is the beginning of Christianity in the life of our nation also, in its history, its culture, its trials.[24]

Pope John Paul II's analysis of this piece of Scripture is amazing. It is something I have not heard even Pentecostal scholars bring to light. When the Holy Spirit fell on the apostles, this signaled that all nations of the earth would hear the gospel of Christ; but the pope takes it one step further. It was not just the contemporary nations of AD 33 that received the promise of the gospel of Christ, but *all* nations that would "enter the Church at different periods and centuries"— Poland being one of those nations, America being one of those nations, Singapore being one of those nations, China being one of those nations, Brazil being among those nations, and every other nation! All nations were to receive the promise of the gospel. **Pentecost is the birth of a Church "for the nations."** You can replace Poland with the name of **your** nation: The day of Pentecost is the

23 Acts 2:5–11 (Berean Study Bible).
24 John Paul II, "Holy Mass." https://www3.nd.edu/~amcadams/
    Communism_2010/PopeinPoland.html

birthday of the faith and of the Church in our land of **America also**. It is the proclamation of the mighty works of God in **our English language also**. It is the beginning of Christianity in the life of our nation also, in its history, its culture, and its trials.

Finally, the pope linked national identity and faith with one final example, this time through the paradigm of the millennium celebration at which he spoke. He was speaking, by God's providence, on the 1,000-year anniversary of the nation.

> To Poland the Church brought Christ, the key to understanding that great and fundamental reality that is man. For man cannot be fully understood without Christ. Or rather, man is incapable of understanding himself fully without Christ. He cannot understand who he is, nor what his true dignity is, nor what his vocation is, nor what his final end is. He cannot understand any of this without Christ. **Therefore Christ cannot be kept out of the history of man in any part of the globe, at any longitude or latitude of geography. The exclusion of Christ from the history of man is an act against man**. It is right to understand the history of the nation through man, each human being of this nation. At the same time man cannot be understood apart from this community that is constituted by the nation. Of course it is not the only community, but it is a special community, perhaps that most intimately linked with the family, the most important for the spiritual history of man. It is therefore impossible without Christ to understand the history of the Polish nation—this great thousand-year-old community—that is so profoundly decisive for me and each one of us. **If we reject this key to understanding our nation, we lay ourselves open to a substantial misunderstanding. We no longer understand ourselves. It is impossible without Christ to understand this nation with its past so full of splendour and also of terrible difficulties.**[25]

---

25 John Paul II, "Holy Mass." https://www3.nd.edu/~amcadams/ Communism_2010/PopeinPoland.html

Like Poland, the nations of the earth, and America in particular, must not reject the key to understanding our national identity hidden in Christ. At the end of his speech, Pope John Paul II prayed on the day of Pentecost, "And I cry—I who am a Son of the land of Poland and who am also Pope John Paul II—I cry from all the depths of this Millennium, I cry on the vigil of Pentecost: **Let your Spirit descend, Let your Spirit descend,** And renew the face of the earth, the face of this land. Amen."[26] At that moment in response, all in the massive crowd lifted up their voices and rang as one voice: "We want God! We want God! We want God!" It was a redeclaration of the Polish spirit, which is a free spirit. And those who were there went home as different people— people who saw themselves not as victims of history, but as witnesses and as strugglers for Christ.

THE ROYAL PRIESTHOOD

The pope's visit to Poland in 1979 was the catalyst that liberated Poland. In the crowds that heard him were the leaders and members of the Solidarity movement, a trade union that would take up the cause of the nation and bring down communism in Poland. Made up of one-third of the country's working population, they led the fight, and it was not that long ago. The conflict intensified as the communist government attempted to destroy the union by imposing martial law from December of 1981 to July 1983. The movement was forced to go underground. Thousands were arrested and put in jail, and many were tortured. It is believed that upwards of ninety-one people were killed during this crackdown. The indispensable man God raised up as the leader of Solidarity was a shipyard electrician named Lech Wałęsa. He would lead the people through the military crackdown and chaos, guiding them from the pope's first visit in 1979 through to Polish independence in 1990, when he was elected president. Wałęsa was given the Nobel Peace Prize in 1983, which raised his stature and probably protected his life from assassination.

Pope John Paul II and Lech Wałęsa fit the pattern we see repeatedly of a governor and a priest working together. We could see this pattern in

---

26 John Paul II, "Holy Mass." https://www3.nd.edu/~amcadams/
  Communism_2010/PopeinPoland.html

the restoration of the temple in Haggai and in the rebuilding of the walls in Nehemiah and Ezra. We also see it in the deliverance of the Jews from the plot of Haman in the first Feast of Purim. Other examples of the code abound.

For instance, in 1953, when Dr. Lester Sumrall[27] visited the Bilibid jail in the Philippines and delivered a young girl from demon possession, the metropolitan radio and press of Manila verified the case, and the world press carried the sensational story. After this miracle, the mayor and officials allowed Dr. Sumrall to conduct meetings that would impact the nation, resulting in the establishment of a 24,000-member church that became the largest congregation in the Philippines at the time.

The alliance of priest and governor occurred again with national impact in 1956 when evangelist Tommy Hicks prayed for the president of Argentina, Juan Peron, who was healed of a skin condition as they prayed. After this, Hicks was given access to Hurricane stadium, where he conducted meetings with 60,000 people, and God seemed to blow in like a hurricane! Night after night, the stadium was filled. Thanks to the powerful combination of the Statesman Evangelist and a government ruler, a strong Christian influence has been permanently embedded in the Philippines and Argentina.

The Statesman Evangelist doesn't always have to be a Billy Graham preaching to hundreds of thousands in stadiums and coliseums. He can be someone like Doug Coe, who was known as the "stealth Billy Graham."[28] President George H.W. Bush called him "the most famous man no one has ever heard of."[29] Doug formed fellowships and small prayer groups in the House, the Senate, the Pentagon, the executive branch, and the judicial branch, and he also formed groups all over the world. He once asked Ward Brim, "If you were God, how would you help all those poor people in Africa?" After confessing he didn't have an answer, Ward heard

27 Sumrall, Lester. Bitten by Devils. (LeSEA Publishing Company, 1987).

28 Wikipedia, "25 Most Influential Evangelicals Photo Essay," Time. July 2, 2005. Archived from the original on April 10, 2010. Retrieved 5/1/2010

29 "Inhofe Honors Doug Coe," YouTube, December 19, 2017, accessed 7/07/2020, www.youtube.com

Doug quietly say, "Change the hearts of the leaders."[30] Doug was a covert Statesman Evangelist with vast influence, both nationally and internationally. Doug traveled literally to every country in the world, bringing leaders together through his quiet, persistent mission to fulfill the great commission of Christ.

What we have learned from the lives of Daniel, Haggai, Zerubbabel, Esther, Lech Wałęsa, Billy Graham, Pope John Paul II, Doug Coe, and many others is that God answers the prayers of his people. He ushers in a deliverer, a Cyrus ruler, or a Statesman Evangelist, but notice in all of these stories that **God's people had to do the work of overthrowing their oppressors.** Though they may be delayed and challenged, there always seems to be a willing remnant who will pay the price to pray and show up where they are needed most. We *"pray for rulers and those that are in authority"* so that we may lead *"godly and peaceable lives."*[31] The prayer part we understand. What else is required? What about a good ruler who does not have sufficient support? *"In a multitude of people is a king's honor, **but in the lack of people is the downfall of a prince.**"*[32]

THE STALLED REFORMATION

This is the point at which we in America must confront our stalled reformation—the house of God has not yet awakened. In Esther's story, deliverance required fasting, prayer, and mobilization at a local and national level. They needed unprecedented unity. Nothing less would enable them to escape the extermination campaign organized against them. The advantage they had over us today is they understood who their common enemy was and the nature of the threat that was organized against them. We have not acquired that level of clarity.

The first serious effort to meet in a corporate call to repentance and intercession for America took place less than forty days before the most critical election of our lifetime. Franklin Graham's prayer march and a two-day event called The Return converged on the nation's Capital on

---

30 Ibid
31 Adapted from 1 Timothy 2:2.
32 Proverbs 14:28

September 26, 2020. As I looked at the crowd of 100,000 Christians assembled together from the Lincoln Memorial to the Washington Monument, I knew that many of them had to sacrifice to make the trip. This was not a gathering of coastal elites. These folks represented the heartbeat of America, and it was clear that they are not willing to melt away into the night. They have urgency in their hearts; and I believe they will someday show up, numbering in the millions, and just like Poland, with one voice declare to the powers gazing at them, "We want God! We want God! We want God!"

CHAPTER 6

THE BATTLE FOR
SHEEP NATIONS

"A nation of sheep will beget a government of wolves."
—*Edward Murrow*

Like never before, we need to hear what the Lord is doing in the midst of providential events affecting America. In the book of Revelation, the writer states: "*Let him who has ears to hear, hear what the Spirit is saying to the church.*"[1] Remember Issachar, the tribe that weighed things past and present to divine the mind of the Lord for what was emerging in the future? They were consulted during a delicate period of political transition in Israel as the house of Saul was on the decline and the house of David was on the rise. Issachar confirmed that it was time to align with the house of David. This is what the Spirit was saying to the tribes. They could see one era of kingdom leadership leaving and a new era beginning. There are a number of sources I use to research what is coming next. In this chapter I want to share two sources that help me get an idea of what "was" and what "is" in order to anticipate "things to come."

---

1 Adapted from Revelation 3:22.

THE CHANGING NATURE OF WARFARE

Let's begin with Rick Joyner, a futurist and one of the top twenty Christian authors of all time. He believes there are four "winds" shaping our period of history.

> In Revelation 7:1 an important paradigm is given that is a key to understanding world history, as well as the present: "After this I saw four angels standing at the four corners of the earth, holding back the four winds of the earth....
>
> Winds often speak of change in literature and Scripture, as in "the winds of change." **History testifies that those who grasp the impact of change are those who will control the future.**
>
> The "four winds of the earth" in Revelation 7:1 are the four great powers that have shaped civilization. These are worldly powers, "winds of the earth," not heaven. Each of these winds dominated one of the four major epochs of world history. They are Military, Religious, Political, and Economic powers. The sequence in which these became dominant saw the construction of civilization in that order.[2]

He describes these four winds as:

- **Military Power:** "Military Power led to the first epoch of recorded history—the age of the conquerors. This period extended from the beginning of recorded history to shortly after the time of Christ. During this age, military leaders were the most powerful men in the world, and military conquests brought about the greatest changes to civilization."[3]

- **Religious Power:** "...Religions that emerged from men, the earth, and not from above. These would include institutional Christianity, Islam, Hinduism, Buddhism, etc. This age extended from about the third century A.D. into the 1500s. During this period, religious leaders were the most powerful men in the world,

---

2 Rick Joyner, "The Winds of Change," Morning Star, Morning Star Fellowship Church, April 24, 2020, https://spe.morningstarministries.org/prophetic-bulletins.

3 Rick Joyner, "The Winds of Change," April 24, 2020.

and the Military became subservient to the Religious powers. Most wars were religious conflicts during this time."[4]

- **Political Power:** "When politics became the most powerful force for change. This began when The Magna Carta was signed, limiting imperial power, and continued into the 20th century. During this period, political changes became the primary change agent in civilization as new forms of government emerged with the social upheavals like the French, American, and Bolshevik revolutions. During this period, the most powerful people were political leaders, and both the religious and military powers became subservient to political power."[5]

- **Economic Power:** "In the late 19th century through the middle of the 20th century, we began to shift into the 4th major civilizational epoch— **the time that would be dominated by economic power.**"[6]

Understanding these "four winds of the earth" can make clear the forces that have shaped the development of civilization, as well as those impacting our own times. Rick explains how over the course of history these different powers have played themselves out.

The Bolshevik Revolution was both a political and an economic revolution, as Marxism is both a political and economic philosophy. World War II was both a political and an economic war, as Japan attacked America because they considered the U.S. economic embargo to be an "act of war." This conflict was the last major repositioning of the nations in preparation for the coming age of economic power.

The "Cold War" was a very real war and the first Economic World War. It only had sporadic and relatively minor military actions. Though political, religious, and military forces remained major powers, the Cold War was different than any previous conflict because it was primarily fought with economic weapons such as banks, currencies, sanctions, and trade policies. Even so, the geopolitical changes brought about by this conflict was as great as any physical war.

---

4 Rick Joyner, "The Winds of Change," April 24, 2020.
5 Rick Joyner, "The Winds of Change," April 24, 2020.
6 Rick Joyner, "The Winds of Change," April 24, 2020.

Winston Churchill foresaw this clash of civilizations based on economics. He also foresaw that it could be won by the West "without having to fire a shot," because Marxist economics cannot compete with the Free Market. President Reagan embraced Churchill's strategy of economic confrontation, and the Iron Curtain did collapse without a shot being fired. The two main globalist forces are Marxism and Islam. Both of these forces have global conquest as a basic doctrine, which the free world has tried to ignore to our great peril.[7]

Understand what Rick is saying here: The war for nations is no longer one dimensional, waged through hand-to-hand combat and ground invasions. Today's war for nations is waged through economic power fought on three fronts: information, technology, and economics. These are the tools of war, and the spoils of victory is control of nations. During this next season, God's house will be visited; and the message of Christ will go forth; kings and nations will be drawn to the light of Christ where it shines brightest. Sheep nations will rise. Now we need to understand how to win this war.

THE GREAT GLOBAL ECONOMIC RESET

As the US economy is left shaking in the aftermath of COVID-19 I asked for perspective from Marc Nuttle—lawyer, author, and economic advisor, who was mentored by Milton Friedman—to explain how economics weaponized to shape nations. Marc explained,

> In January 2020, prior to the pandemic, 52.5 percent of the American adult population received their primary income via a direct check from a government entity: 19 percent welfare, 3.5 percent unemployment, 18 percent work for a government entity, and 12 percent Social Security. Theoretically, none of these citizens experienced any change in income during the shutdown.
>
> The Federal Reserve Board estimates chronic unemployment will settle in at 8.5 percent. An increase of 5 percent unemployment could bring the public to 57.5 percent receiving a direct check

---

7   Rick Joyner, "The Winds of Change," April 24, 2020.

from the government for primary income. Sixty percent is a warning threshold.

In January of 2021, it is estimated that the United States government will be $30 trillion in debt, borrowed against a $20 trillion economy. One hundred fifty percent (150%) debt to GDP is beyond any matrix or chart now used by economists for projecting economic stability. If, in fact, the structural unemployment rate is 8.5 percent, we will be precariously close to a tipping point of societal/government economic relationship.

By necessity, government is establishing a reverse domino effect. A moratorium on tenant evictions has been set by several states. Landlords require leniency from banks to pay their notes. Banks are now lobbying the FDIC for relaxation of requirements to allow nonperforming real estate assets to be held on their books for an extended period of time. The federal government then permits certain banks to operate with dead assets.

Each of these actions eliminates a traditional course of correction to economic restructuring. Normally, tenants would have been removed and replaced with others who can pay rent. Banks would have foreclosed on landlords. Properties would have been rehabilitated for more efficient economic returns. Banks would have been required to write down bad loans and therefore forced to reexamine lending policies or fail.

An economic reset and restructuring are certain. This reverse domino effect that has been established because of the pandemic crisis must be managed so that the ultimate reset is not socialism, Marxism, or communism.

What is paramount is an absolute commitment to finding solutions in our economic chaos through free-enterprise principles. Not for the purpose of maintaining power with any group, but to maintain freedom for all groups.

Without freedom, hope is lost. Without hope, perseverance is lost. Without perseverance, free will is lost. Without free will, one's soul is lost.

While government programs are necessary, government jobs are critical to an ordered society. We need elected officials and their staff to run the country. The military, police, and county sheriffs provide safety. The essential nature and importance of all categories of government expenditure are not the point. The point is that, at a certain level of citizen dependence upon a government check, the private sector is not able to support the level of government spending. At this tipping point, the only solution is a collapse into total government control, resulting in elimination of private ownership and redistribution of wealth.

Recently, Alexandria Ocasio-Cortez (AOC), a progressive leader, called for government restructuring encompassing many policies of socialism at the least, and Marxism at the worst. Black Lives Matter has agreed with AOC in part in its call for reforms to achieve racial equality.

More money is the recurring chorus. If governments could just print money and distribute it to whomever they desired, they would have done it a long time ago. Venezuela would do it today. Why haven't they? Because it doesn't work. For every government economic action, there is always an equal and opposite economic reaction. This may be inflation, deflation, or a debasement of the currency. Under no economic system can you just print money forever.

The people of the United States want racial reconciliation, fairness, and universal equality. Neither socialism nor communism, under the aegis of Marxism, is the proper economic structure to reach the goal of egalitarianism. One only has to examine the lessons of history, past and current, to acknowledge the failures of totalitarianism.

Socialism is the concept that, in the elimination of private ownership, the people own everything collectively and are left to make choices by societal demand for production and consumption. Marxism takes all choices away from the people and decides by government edict the goals and priorities of both production and consumption.

What progressives neglect to recognize is that, in socialism and communism, the people's choices for pursuit of happiness are restricted to the options offered by an elitist group of government managers and dictators. A person has little freedom to make individual choices of destiny for himself or herself and their families. The equal outcome is the goal, regardless of how universally bleak or demeaning the eventual standard of living becomes.[8]

When Vladimir Lenin came to power in Russia in 1917, he saw his key to power as the removal of privately owned property. All belonged to the state. By the time of his death seven years later, he had seen --and strongly stressed --the power of a huge bureaucratic socialist government. Private property would give way to the big government organization as a source of power. This is important, because the emerging socialism in America is less about government running businesses as it is about government expanding power to enforce rules reinforcing the application of cultural Marxism to churches, businesses, schools, and all private associations—much in the same way the homosexual community dismantled the Boy Scouts.

> "WHAT PROGRESSIVES NEGLECT TO RECOGNIZE IS THAT, IN SOCIALISM AND COMMUNISM, THE PEOPLE'S CHOICES FOR PURSUIT OF HAPPINESS ARE RESTRICTED TO THE OPTIONS OFFERED BY AN ELITIST GROUP OF GOVERNMENT MANAGERS AND DICTATORS."
> —MARC NUTTLE.

In terms of economic socialism we are dangerously close to the point of no return. In order to get the debt under control, Trump in 2016 first had to reinvigorate the economy, bring jobs home, and increase US-based production so we would once again have a strong GDP. Think of GDP as all the money you make in a given year. The national debt is just like your normal household debt. For almost thirty years, we have seen the national debt go from 4 trillion to 26 trillion—there was unprecedented spending under Bush and Obama. Now, we have hit a national emergency and just wrote another 2.8 trillion[9] to pay for COVID expenses. Progressives want trillions more

---

8   Marc Nuttle. Personal Interview. 2020.

9   Drew Desilver, "The U.S. Budget Deficit Is Rising Amid COVID-19, But Public Concern About It Is Falling." Pew Research Center, August 13, 2020, https://www.

to bail out the failing blue states that are continuing to run cities into the ground. This would never work in your household budget. If you are spending more than you're making, you will eventually run out of credit and lose everything you own. This is basically where we are with the growing national debt, bloated government programs, and lack of small business owners to pay taxes into the system to keep it afloat.

Just as you have to pay VISA or Mastercard each month, the US has different entities that hold its debt. Would it surprise you to find out other countries own large portions of our debt?

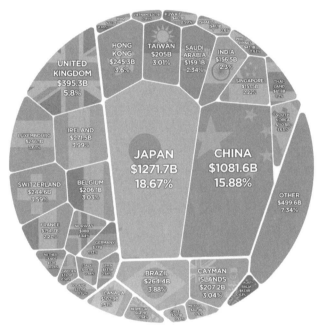

Foreign Holders of U.S. Debt 2020 [10]
Countries Owning U.S. Debt in Billions of Dollars & Percentage

*Data as of March 2020
Article and Sources:
https://howmuch.net/articles/foreign-holders-of-us-debt-2020
U.S. Department of the Treasury · https://home.treasury.gov

howmuch .net

pewresearch.org/fact-tank/2020/08/13 /the-u-s-budget-deficit-is-rising-amid-covid-19-but-public-concern-about-it-is-falling/.

10 Irena Editor, Irena, and Editor. "Charted: The Biggest Foreign Holders of U.S. Debt." HowMuch. howmuch.net, June 1, 2020. https://howmuch.net/articles/foreign-holders-of-us-debt-2020.

Eventually we will get to a point where we can't even pay the interest on the debt. Just like with your credit cards, if you do not pay, the debt collectors start calling and your credit rating begins to take a hit. In the case of America, the world will take notice (since we owe them payments) and the thing that will take a hit is the United States dollar! Globally, there is the risk that countries will no longer feel confident in the dollar as the world's reserve currency. As a result, they may switch to one or a combination of the other four reserve currencies: the euro, British pound sterling, Japanese yen, and Chinese yuan.

If that happens, our dollar will become the Venezuelan bolívar, and we will be buying bread with a wheelbarrow full of money. Why? Because all that money we printed, the trillions and trillions of dollars, will come home to the US as countries now move to a new currency to buy and sell. This isn't as far fetched as it seems; eventually all currencies at some point either become devalued or collapse. The most likely scenario to come to pass is rapidly rising debt and rising inflation.

The only other scenario to officially forecast is the rise of a digital currency, backed by some sort of commodity. A digital currency, also known as cryptocurrency, will be the future, because it's the confluence of technology, information, and economics. Wikipedia has a easy to understand definition of what a cryptocurrency is:

> "A crypto currency is a digital asset designed to work as a medium of exchange wherein individual coin ownership records are stored in a ledger existing in a form of a computerized database using strong cryptography [called blockchain] to secure transaction records, to control the creation of additional coins, and to verify the transfer of coin ownership. It typically does not exist in physical form (like paper money) and is usually not issued by a central authority. Cryptocurrencies rely on decentralized control, as opposed to central banking systems."[11]

This is appealing because it reduces corruption, provides accountability and stops the arbitrary creation of new money. While that can be a lot to

---

11 "Cryptocurrency." Wikipedia. Wikimedia Foundation, September 20, 2020. https://en.wikipedia.org/wiki/Cryptocurrency.

take in, the summary is that it is an innovative way to buy and sell goods and services without government control. This is being used now by early adopters but will be mainstream, probably within five to ten years. Nations—like China and the EU—are already talking about creating digital currencies.

The other component we could see developed is a digital token that will be a combination of your Social Security number, passport, and medical history that is assigned to you at birth, holding all of your financial, legal, and personal information. It could also be coded to verify that you have been properly vaccinated or not vaccinated. This is no longer the stuff of end-time fiction. The removal of a physical currency will cascade into a number of issues that will only bring us closer to what the book of Revelation predicts.

For Christians with an ear to hear, this period of chaos is also chaordic. *Chaordic*[12] is the word created by Dee Hock, the inventor of Visa and Mastercard, when he began to envision a world where a plastic card could be a global currency. Chaordic refers to the opportunity that develops in the midst of chaos. For those who can disconnect from the shaking and press into the realm the Bible describes as *"a kingdom that cannot be shaken,"*[13] there will be exploits and opportunities. I know of Christians who are developing new trading platforms and even some that are creating their own Christian cryptocurrency, so when the day arrives that we can no longer buy and sell with the world's funds, we will have an alternative way to do business.

WHEN NATIONS AND CORPORATIONS CONSPIRE

The reality is, the battle for nations is being fought on many fronts. It is not just governments behind the manipulation of economics, but also major companies. Plenty of corporations outpace some of the largest economies in the world. Did you know that Walmart generates more revenue than Spain and Australia? Walmart's 482 billion dollars exceeds Spain's 461 billion and Australia's 421 billion. When you overlay the top 100 revenue-generating nation states and corporations we find out seventy-one out of the 100 are corporations!

---

12 Dee Hock, "Chaordic Age Organizations." Dee W Hock, 2020,
    http://www.deewhock.com/essays
13 Hebrews 12:28 (ESV).

Country/Corporations	Rev. (US Billions)	Country [14]
1. United States	3363	
2. China	2465	
3. Japan	1696	
4. Germany	1507	
5. France	1288	
6. United Kingdom	996	
7. Italy	843	
8. Brazil	632	
9. Canada	595	
10. Walmart	482	US
11. Spain	461	
12. Australia	421	
13. State Grid	330	CH
14. Netherlands	323	
15. South Korea	304	
16. China Nat. Petroleum	299	CH
17. Sinopec Group	294	CH
18. Royal Dutch Shell	272	GB/NL
19. Sweden	248	
20. Exxon Mobile	246	US
21. Volkswagon	237	DE
22. Toyota Motor	237	JP
23. Apple	234	US
24. Belgium	232	
25. BP	226	GB
26. Mexico	224	
27. Switzerland	216	
28. Berkshire Hathaway	211	US
29. India	200	
30. Norway	200	

*BASED ON FORBES FORTUNE GLOBAL 500 LIST 2017 AND. CIA WORLD FACTBOOK 2017.

COUNTRIES VS CORPORATIONS

14 Authors' calculation based on Forbes Fortune Global 500 list 2017 and CIA World Factbook 2017.

We need to understand that American companies, like Exxon, are not making decisions based on how they help America. Rather, they are looking to generate profits and avoid taxes. They much prefer a globalist world where they can incorporate in one country, manufacture in another, and do banking in a third. Can you see how Donald Trump has messed up their game? His one goal is to make American manufacturing great again and get better-paying jobs for American workers. Global big business, on the other hand, wants endless immigration, which provides cheap labor. A borderless world with no tariffs, where workers can cross with ease from one country to another. They are looking to build a world where they are able to make money more efficiently, even if it is at the expense of nations' economies or sovereignty.

The fact that companies are as influential as nations should reshape how we see corporations. Nations now compete with corporations for influence and political power. International relations has become a giant multi-dimensional chess game, with nations and corporations as intertwined actors. What happens when big business and nations start putting together their own plan for the world? To answer this question, we need to take a look *across the pond* at Europe, because that is exactly what is happening over there at Davos, and it will impact us.

Davos is the name of a city in Switzerland where the world's most influential people, European government officials, intellectual elites, and the CEOs of large international corporations gather to collaborate over the world's economic and political challenges. The formal name for this gathering is the World Economic Forum (WEF). It was established in the early 1970s by Klaus Schwab.

Each year, business leaders and heads of state give lectures and speak on panels about topics ranging from gender equality and venture capital to mental health and climate change. Marc Nuttle says, "Attendance at the annual conference is strictly by invitation only. Billionaires, Hollywood elites, and Fortune 500 CEOs assemble at the Forum in a resemblance of the Versailles Balls of the early twentieth century. There are no small family-owned businesses represented at the WEF in Davos."[15] Strategic Partners pay in excess of $500,000 to $600,000 per year to be listed as members.

15 Marc Nuttle. Personal Interview. 2020.

The World Economic Forum, "is funded by its 1,000 member companies, typically global enterprises with more than five billion dollars in turnover ... These enterprises rank among the top companies within their industry and/or country and play a leading role in shaping the future of their industry and/or region. Membership is stratified by the level of engagement with forum activities, with the level of membership fees increasing as participation in meetings, projects, and initiatives rises. In 2011 an annual membership cost $52,000 for an individual member, $263,000 for an "Industry Partner," and $527,000 for a "Strategic Partner."[16]

Marc continues:

> One of the Forum's earliest consortium projects was to establish the United States of Europe. This, in fact, led to exchequers from key European capitals planning for the establishment of the European Union (EU) and the issuance of the Euro as a universal composite currency. The EU, of course, became reality. However, economic policy has continued to be their bane.
>
> The Davos collection of intellectuals includes many billionaires who, through the Forum, have actually acted as a super legislature in proposing world government policy. Even though the EU struggles with government debt, growth in GDP, and social policy, the WEF has now moved on to emphasize global warming as their key concern. **The Davos Forum is now calling for a Great Reset.** This reset involves **completely restructuring capitalism,** coordinated through government policy, for more desired outcomes. **Former US Vice President Al Gore** has called for a meeting of nations to impose new mandatory guidelines for climate control. Inclusive in the reset is the recalibration of currencies, the rescheduling of debt, and the reset of priorities for world coordination of government and corporate mandates. This call for a world convocation requires all nations to attend. **The goal is a one-world regulatory authority. Any nations**

---

16 "World Economic Forum," September 10, 2020. https://en.wikipedia.org/wiki/ World_Economic_Forum.

not agreeing to the accords become a competition and therefore a threat to the new ruling order.

The question begging to be addressed is, in all of this effort by WEF to produce wage equality, redistribution of wealth, access to capital, and climate control, who is the watchman of individual liberty?

Right now, the world's global elites are advancing their policy agendas unopposed, without resistance from communities and governments that claim free will and freedom as the essence of their existence. Yes, the pandemic has and will change the order of world economics and government policy forever. And the social fabric of families will be impacted. How that change and impact is managed depends on how and what options are presented for the public's determination. The citizens' decisions about future government structure will be the next generations' inheritance.

This Davos Challenge necessitates an answer. Davos is operating unchallenged as a predominantly unelected elitist group believing that, in their combined intellect, they know what is best for mankind. This type of arrogance has always resulted in totalitarianism, knowing only failure as its legacy.[17]

THE EU GAME OF THRONES

Davos transnational corporations, the EU, China, and progressives all aspire to control nations. What do they have in common? They are all jockeying for position in a global game of thrones. In the end this is an economic war, and the battle is for control of sovereign nations. In the midst of this, sheep and goat nations will be defined.

The EU was moving forward until it encountered the wrecking ball of Donald Trump and Boris Johnson. These two leaders emerged as a populous backlash against the control of globalist elites. US citizens sent a message to Washington, and the Brits sent a message to Brussels. The emerging sheep nations of Europe want European unity, but they want it based on distinct national identities grounded in a shared classical and Christian civilization. They see the threat of globalism and do not want the creation of a super-state using technology to create a single economic

---

17 Marc Nuttle. Personal Interview. 2020.

and political system. They want economic security, but not at the price of losing their unique national identity or defiling their culture.

Johnson is setting things up for a hard exit from the EU. It's not in the UK's best interest financially or politically to be tied into the EU. The EU needs British money, but the British do not need the EU. Johnson is watching the 2020 US election with keen interest. He and Trump are ready to go full tilt in a free-trade agreement, starting January 1, 2021, and it will rock the investment world to the advantage of both nations. If the US and UK team up, they can, together, act like trade rivals to the EU.

The lockdowns due to COVID-19 provided perfect relief to the EU, because a weak British economy undermines Johnson's hard Brexit exit. The EU is like China in the sense that it wants to use the COVID-19 crisis to remake itself into a super state. The EU wants to run an independent central bank that has full monetary power over all its subordinated member states—like Sauron's ring in Tolkien's classic, "one bank to rule them all."[18]

To understand the EU, think of the fifty states in the US and imagine that each state had its own central bank and printed money whenever it wanted to. Texas, for instance, would have a fit if Michigan discovered that the shutdown of its economy moved the state to the brink of bankruptcy, and decided to print trillions to bail itself out. That's the dynamic between Germany and Italy (Germany being Texas); Germany doesn't want to be responsible for Italy's debt.

What is happening right now in the EU is even worse. The European Central Bank is using the COVID-19 crisis to propose a multi-trillion-euro quantitative easing plan. Quantitative easing is designed to *ease* the pressure on the economy by controlling the *quantity* of money in the market. It is a fancy way of saying, "We are going into the basement in Brussels to print more money and infuse it into the economy." The EU needs to print money like Washington prints money, because what they are doing economically isn't working.

This is why Brussels must keep the UK locked into the EU boondoggle—because once free from the mess in Europe, money would flow to London and the US as an alternative destination for capital. The last thing the EU wants is the UK looking like a greater success after leaving

---

18 J.R.R. Tolkien, *The Lord of the Rings* (New York: Del Rey/Ballantine Books, 2012).

the marriage. They want Boris Johnson to fail gloriously. His departure is exposing deep fault lines in the EU. For this reason, it is working melo-dramatically to make the case that COVID-19 requires a whole reset of all economies, globally.

Now you have an understanding of what we are up against. **The battlefield for nations is fought through economic warfare.** As the battle rages, the decisive fight we must win will be election day 2020. The next few months are the most important months in the history of Europe and the US. If Brexit is successfully derailed and Trump is deposed, **then get ready to watch the European Union rise** from life support to take its place on the throne.

RESPECT THESE
SOVEREIGN SPHERES

With all that said, why do we fight in the economic war happening around us? Christians are, by and large, a submissive and accommodating group. However, there is a point where governments and corporations can go too far and force Christians to transgress their conscience. It's at this point we tread into the uncharted territory of civil disobedience, like the first-century Church when disciples were arrested for preaching. Peter and John said: *"Whether it is right in the sight of God to listen to you rather than to God, you must judge, for we cannot but speak of what we have seen and heard."*[19] When the apostles were brought to trial a second time, the Sanhedrin told them: *"'We gave you strict orders not to teach in this name yet you have filled Jerusalem with your teaching and are determined to make us responsible for this man's* [Jesus's] *blood."*[20] But Peter and the other apostles replied, *"'We must obey God rather than men.'"*[21]

Notice the principle? Jesus taught the disciples to *"render to Caesar what is Caesar's and to God what is God's."*[22] They understood that the government has a sphere. These men were willing to die, and would die,

---

19 Acts 4:19 (ESV).
20 Acts 5:28 (ESV).
21 Acts 5:29 (ESV).
22 Mark 12:17 (Berean Study Bible).

rather than disobey God's call to preach. This point of contention between government and religion comes down to conflicting spheres of jurisdiction. It answers the question: who has ultimate authority? There are five clear spheres of sovereignty designed by God where Christ and heaven's ordinances, principles, and designs are intended to operate independent of outside control:

1. Personal
2. Church
3. Family
4. Government
5. Business and voluntary associations

God's Word lays out principles that help each person understand his or her authority, responsibility, and accountability to God. These are individual gardens where God walks in the cool of the day to commune with His people as they cultivate what is in their hand. Parents, for instance, are to rule their household and provide for and raise their children. Managers should be diligent in business and generous in wages. Church elders are to feed and nurture the Church, being accountable to God for the flock. Each realm has a design and boundaries. The Ten Commandments warn of coveting, or desiring to take another man's property. There are boundaries to behavior. These boundaries are sacred to God, and the overreach of one domain into another produces hardship, confusion, and often destruction. *"There is a time in which one man rules over another to his own hurt."*[23] Who has the ultimate authority to rule your family? Teach your children? Shut down your business or tell you what kind of work you can or cannot do? **The realm of government has a place, and man has an obligation to respect the government; but the realm of conscience and obedience to God is a higher obligation.** The apostles did not submit to the Sanhedrin, because the Jewish court did not have greater authority than God. Like the Sanhedrin, governments and corporations overreach beyond their sovereign sphere when they violate the sovereignty of individuals, parents, pastors, and business owners.

---

23 Ecclesiastes 8:9 (NKJV).

One of the great architects of Christian thought regarding culture and how these spheres overlap was Abraham Kuyper (1837–1920). Kuyper was one of the most extraordinary individuals of his time. A prolific intellectual and theologian, he founded a newspaper and a university and was instrumental in church reformation. He was also an active politician, serving as a member of Parliament in the Netherlands beginning in 1874, and serving as prime minister from 1901 to 1905.

Kuyper explains the role of spheres and government this way:

> All these spheres interlock like cogwheels, and precisely in acting upon one another and in meshing with one another, they produce the rich, multifaceted variety of human society. But this also brings the danger that one sphere in life may break in upon another like a jerky cogwheel that shears off one cog after another until the operation of the entire machine is disrupted. This danger constitutes the rationale for still another sphere of authority, that of the state. The state must make it possible for the various spheres, insofar as they manifest themselves externally, to interact appropriately, and to keep each sphere within its proper limits… The state is a sovereign power…which protects the individual from the tyranny of his own group. It has no authority, however, within each of these five spheres. Internally, each sphere is ruled by another authority that descends directly from God, apart from the state.[24]

America's founders shared a worldview similar to Kuyper's; and they knew that man is corruptible and would require a checks-and-balances system to govern. They embedded in America's founding documents the fundamental truth that *the state cannot give man his freedoms.* The American Declaration of Independence espouses this idea: "We hold these truths to be self-evident, that all men are created equal, that they are endowed by their Creator with certain unalienable Rights, that among these are Life, Liberty and the pursuit of Happiness."[25] Man's freedoms and rights come only from his Creator.

---

24 Terry M. Crist, *Learning the Language of Babylon:* (U.S.: Xulon Press, 2004).
25 National Archives. https://www.archives.gov/founding-docs/declaration-transcript

STORMY WINDS FULFILLING HIS WORD

It is likely that the four winds Rick Joyner writes about—military, political, religious, and economic—will all converge at some point in the future. Jesus said in the last days, "You will hear of wars and rumors of wars, but see to it that you are not alarmed. Such things must happen, but the end is still to come. Nation will rise against nation, and kingdom against kingdom."[26]

As heaven comes down and nations shake in the midst of all that, the gospel of the kingdom will increase in power as it goes forth—reaping a global harvest and sovereign nations, sheep nations that will have Cyrus "kings" who come to the light of Christ's rising.

While political and cultural Marxism is resurging, radical Islam is still a threat. Islam is seen by many as a religion; but it is, in reality, a political idea wrapped in a religious garment. Remember, Rick said, "The two main globalist forces are Communism and Islam. Both of these forces have global conquest as a basic doctrine."[27] In terms of the anatomy of power, these forces will dominate, intimidate, and control, whereas Christians shape the environment by persuasion. The Word of the Lord will go forth with increased power as the winds of the Spirit counter the four winds of the earth: military, political, religious and economic.

Arise, shine, for your light has come, and the glory of the LORD rises upon you. For behold, darkness covers the earth, and thick darkness is over the peoples; but the LORD will rise upon you, and His glory will appear over you. Nations will come to your light, and kings to the brightness of your dawn.[28]

Many see this verse as being fulfilled when the Lord returns to rule from Jerusalem in His messianic kingdom, but this does not explain why there is "thick darkness covering the people." This can only describe a time when heaven and hell have intensified their occupation of the earth. The "glory of the Lord" referred to by Isaiah is the same as the glory prophesied by Haggai saying, "*the glory of this latter house shall be greater than*

---

26 Matthew 24:6–8 (NIV).
27 Rick Joyner, "The Winds of Change," April 24, 2020.
28 Isaiah 60:1–2 (Berean Study Bible).

the former." This will occur as the Lord is rising upon the Church, the *"one new man"*[29] made up of Jewish and Gentile believers. This verse covers the transition from the end of this age to the beginning of Messiah's reign. In all the shaking of heaven and earth, the people of God will be *"receiving a kingdom which cannot be moved."*[30] The writer adds, *"Let us have grace* [a steady current of divine enablement] *whereby we may serve God acceptably with reverence and godly fear: For our God is a consuming fire."*[31] A true awakening is overtaking a fake awakening, and the fire of God is countering the fire of a counterfeit movement.

If you would like to hear more from Marc and Rick about the unfolding economic battle for nations please visit GodChaosCode.com/Thrones

---

29 Ephesians 2:15 (NKJV).
30 Hebrews 12:28 (KJV).
31 Hebrews 12:28–29 (KJV).

CHAPTER 7

THE NEW RELIGION

"Christians should give more offense, shock the
world far more, than they are doing now."
— *George Orwell*

"Lance, is that your limo burning?" I had just come up the escalator of the Reagan Building in Washington, DC, with my wife Annabelle to watch the inauguration parade. People were gathered around a TV, looking at news coverage. I came over to see what the commotion was about.

The vehicle was now wrapped in billowing flames as smoke poured through the shattered windows. I saw swarms of people vandalizing the

I prayed that fire would fall. I should have been more specific.

car, all dressed in black, wearing masks, and armed with bricks and spray paint. My thoughts quickly turned to the driver. *Is he safe?*

As I was trying to process all the chaos, a text arrived. The businessman who graciously provided us with the limo told me about all the trauma the driver had gone through to escape. He saw the Antifa mob, and they saw him—then the violence started. He saw the brick fly through the window just in time to throw up his arms and protect his head. With his arm now smashed, he opened the driver-side door, dove out, and escaped just in time to see the vehicle burst into flames. I read that text and just couldn't believe it. Just minutes before, we were sitting in the back seat!

This was my official introduction to the chaos of the radicalized left— namely Antifa—a festive group that believes no party is complete without Molotov cocktails. By firebombing the limo, Antifa destroyed the livelihood of three people—the African American and Hispanic drivers we'd had for two days and the Muslim owner who hoped this transportation service would be an opportunity to make a living in America. Rather than prosper the cause, Antifa terrorists created well over $100,000 in destruction with one act. The irony is that Antifa claims to be anti-capitalist while they consistently destroy minority-owned businesses in the path of their "peaceful protests" (as CNN puts it).

WE HAVE BEEN HIJACKED

The growing Trumpian Psychosis, Black Lives Matter movement (BLM), and the Democratic party have reached a murky pinnacle in the US. Think of America as an airplane flight. It was designed so that every four years, that plane lands and the passengers get to vote on who they want in the cockpit and cabin crew for the next four years. However, this current flight we are on is different; we are in danger, and you can feel it in your gut.

This flight is being taken over by a highly radicalized minority of people on the passenger list who are holding the entire plane hostage, like four men with box cutters trying to barge into the cabin. It only takes a small group of organized terrorists to take over a flight and crash the plane, especially if the passengers and crew are unaware of the threat and unprepared to protect themselves. Civilized people don't think the same way as suicide bombers.

Many Americans feel like a cultural 9/11 is unfolding in front of them but have no clue that a radicalized ideology has taken us all captive. To regain control, we are going to need to understand how we got here and what we are currently facing.

THE NEW RELIGION

Decades ago, Dr. Carl F. Henry, the founder and editor of *Christianity Today*, sent a questionnaire to individuals he deemed "twenty of the leading intellectual preachers in the country." Dr. Henry asked these notable minds, "What do you see for the church of Jesus Christ by the year 2000."[1] Elton Trueblood, a noted twentieth-century American Quaker author and theologian, and former chaplain both to Harvard and Stanford universities, responded quite prophetically saying, "By the year 2000, Christians in America will be a conscious minority, surrounded by an arrogant, militant paganism."[2] All you need to do is turn on the news to see how accurate Trueblood's words were.

This "new religion" of militant paganism, referred to by scholars as *Secular Fundamentalism,* has taken over the Democratic Party. At its summer meeting on August 24, 2019, in San Francisco, California, the Democratic National Committee (DNC) passed a resolution praising the values of "religiously unaffiliated" Americans and recognizing them as the "largest religious group within the Democratic Party." The resolution, which was unanimously passed, was championed by the *Secular Coalition of America*, an organization that lobbies on behalf of atheists, agnostics, and humanists on public policy. The group celebrated the DNC's move as the first time a major party "embraced American nonbelievers."[3] This explains why at their 2020 convention they dropped the reference to God in the pledge of allegiance, removing "Under God."

Yet, like a mental virus hatched out of a satanic bioweapons lab, a new species of *Secular Fundamentalism* has mutated into existence. It's called

---

1 Henry, Carl F, quoted by Leonard Ravenhill in *Sodom Had No Bible* (Bloomington: Bethany House, 1988), 13.

2 Trueblood, Elton, quoted by Leonard Ravenhill in *Sodom Had No Bible* (Bloomington: Bethany House, 1988), 13.

3 Secular Coalition of America, "Democratic Party embraces nonreligious voters at annual summer meeting." August 26, 2019, https://secular.org/2019/08/democratic-party-embraces-nonreligious-voters-at-annual-summer-meeting/

Progressive Fundamentalism, and it's far more dangerous. The difference is, secular fundamentalist liberals and agnostics, like Bill Maher and Sam Harris, express open contempt for "simpletons" in the faith community, but they can live with them. Not so with progressive fundamentalists; the very beliefs of the faith community are, in their minds, an assault on what they hold sacred. They cannot coexist. They are obligated to purge that which is impure.

THE NEW SACRED

In every religion there are three fundamental elements: sacred objects, a unified set of beliefs and practices, and the existence of a moral community. Of the three, perhaps the most important would be the notion of "the sacred," which is the point around which any religious system revolves.

The "sacred" is that which inspires great respect and admiration on the part of society and what is set apart and keeps believers united. For Christians, this would be Jesus and the Bible; for the Jew, it would be Moses and the Torah; for Muslims, it would be the prophet Muhammad and the Koran.

Émile Durkheim, a French sociologist who rose to prominence in the late nineteenth and early twentieth centuries, helped shape awareness of what societies deem sacred. Durkheim's definition of religion was: "A unified system of beliefs and practices relative to sacred things, that is to say, things set apart and forbidden—beliefs and practices which unite in one single moral community called a Church, all those who adhere to them." [4]

To Durkheim, the sacred does not have to be a divine or supernatural being. The sacred is anything viewed as "exalted" or "set apart," anything that provides definition and meaning to a larger community. Once the sacred is discovered in a moral community, you know what a person really values and, in a sense, worships.

This is, in fact, the central element of what is happening in America. Consider with me the spiritual crossroads we are facing as a nation. On

---

4 Durkheim, Emile. "The Elementary Forms of the Religious Life." (Sage Publications Inc., 1986) https://durkheim.uchicago.edu/Summaries/forms. html.

one side, homosexuality is a sin; on the other, thinking of homosexuality as sin translates as "intolerance" or "discrimination" against lesbians, gays, bisexuals, and transgenders. The same with abortion, with immigration, and with the Second Amendment.

To put this in the language of Émile Durkheim, what is ultimately being decided are conflicting conceptions of what is sacred. Each side of America's cultural divide operates with a different concept of what is sacred, and the mere existence of one represents a certain desecration of the other.

THE NEW SIN

Now, reframe *Progressive Fundamentalism* through the lens of Durkheim's research. Does the left hold anything sacred? Consider how the left deals with a "sin" or "misdeed": an errant tweet, joke, old college photo, or Facebook post carries a harsh judgment if it offends the sacred. Oftentimes, this costs the offender his or her career and livelihood. Cancel culture is the favorite tool for excommunication in *Progressive Fundamentalism*.

This is a religion devoid of forgiveness, with the only path to redemption being a very public verbal flagellation and apology for going against the sacred. There are acts that cannot be performed, words that cannot be said, and thoughts that cannot be thought. Like a cult, members must constantly investigate themselves and each other—in order to ensure their purity. Enemies of the cult must be vilified and persecuted as an expression of devotion. This negative focus is what makes it so vindictive and combative. In order to advance what is sacred, non-believers are the object of aggressive vigilance. The movement must be protected from pollution by the politically incorrect, who are considered profane.

THE NEW CONFESSION

Of course, free speech is upheld in the church of *Progressive Fundamentalism*—just so long as it is "politically correct" speech. The new religion is highly sensitive to anything that sounds like "blasphemy."

To understand the laws regarding speech in the new religion, you need to know why the left will shout you down and disrupt you when you try to reason with them. They will tell you that you do not understand the situation. Then, if you try to speak, you will be cut off because you are incapable of saying anything intelligible since you do not understand. You are told that you need to listen because of your "sin"—your religion, whiteness, straightness, or maleness. These are not sins of behavior; they are sins of design.

The left's attacks on religious freedom and general hatred for those who don't agree with them is driven by "identity politics." Identity politics happens when people form political alliances not based on political ideals but rather on race, gender, or sexual orientation. It is important to understand identity politics because they are being weaponized to divide America.

The recent rise in identity politics wasn't accidental. It was actually contrived as a solution for the failing Democratic recruitment tool—unions. Once a reliable and growing voting group, unions plateaued as the technology industries took over where manufacturing once reigned. Where would Democrats find new groups of underrepresented people? For centuries, Marxists would try to pit the working class against the rich; but that wasn't working in America, where we have a strong economy, a contented middle class, and record low unemployment numbers. They found an answer: identity politics.

Democrats would cobble together a constituency by atomizing society into different interest groups according to sexual preference, gender, race, or any combination in a hierarchy of oppressed people. If the other party is made of married heterosexual couples, they will make this family arrangement, the nuclear family, the oppressive enemy of their story. If white male evangelicals are a part of the Republican party, the white male patriarchy checks off the box and justifies both the attack on the nuclear family and white males in general. Women's liberation groups, activists, and lesbians found an ally in this new coalition.

Seeing the world through the lens of inequality provides a convenient and morally attractive way for youth to crusade for a world of peace and inequity on earth. It is brilliant branding, as the term itself sets up the question "Are you opposed to social justice?" This is a prescription for true oppression, as the government steps in to create "social justice" by depriving those who are not part of the new "union's" collective bargaining tactics and redistributing to those who are "victims." It is a prescription for ongoing, exacerbated, irreconcilable conflict and division. New words like "homophobia," "white privilege," "xenophobia," "islamophobia," and "transphobia" became common. These topics are not only taught in universities, but they are also embedded in social media companies that have joined the crusade and have the power to direct what most people know, think, and say. In this sense, the new cultural Marxism is not terribly far from the logic and indoctrination of the Nazis against the Jewish people. The Jews were branded as the reason for all of Germany's—and the world's—ills. Identity politics is the vehicle for groups to organize and acquire power over middle-class values, and the Republican party in particular.

The rules for speech in the new fundamentalism are interesting. Its members are believers in policing free speech and enforcing "compelled speech," also a tool of Marxist indoctrination. It is nothing less than the repudiation of the First Amendment of the Constitution and the very foundation of Western Civilization. Free speech deals with what comes out of your mouth; compelled speech puts words into your mouth. The new religion will force you to say what they want you to say, even if you do not believe it. This is a dangerous line to cross, and it's already been crossed and bled into American institutions of government. The US Army maintains an "Equity and Inclusion Agency," where anti-American indoctrination has worked its way from academia into the vital tissues of culture. Its seminar, Operation Inclusion, instructs its students—US Army personnel—that "voicing support for enforcing immigration laws or repeating phrases such as 'Make America Great Again' are evidence of white supremacy."[5] You are a racist if you think that "All Lives Matter." You are in denial if you do not recognize "white privilege," and if you support "Columbus Day" or believe in the idea of "American exceptionalism"[6] (which is simply the belief that God and not the State rules over the people, and the people get to choose who they believe should serve in government). In essence, progressive fundamentalists believe, "God is not a factor in the citizens' participation in government 'of the people, by the people and for the people.'"[7] The consultants running this training have penetrated the upper echelon of

---

5   "Equity and Inclusion Agency." *US Army*, 2020, https://www.asamra.army.mil/org_diversity.html.

6   Kimball, Roger. "The White Supremacy Phantom." *The Spectator*, 2019, https://spectator.us/white-supremacy-phantom/.

7   *Americans United for Separation of Church and State*, 2020. "Operation Inclusion." https://www.au.org/content/operation-inclusion.

the Treasury Department, the Federal Reserve, the Federal Deposit Insurance Corporation, the Consumer Financial Protection Bureau, the Office of the Comptroller, the Department of Justice, the National Institute of Health, and the Office of the Attorney General. Obviously, the bureaucratic state (or deep state) agenda had already begun making converts to its agenda when its training reached the military.[8] Donald Trump discovered what was going on and put a stop to it. The Biden–Harris administration will kick it back into high gear if given power.

THE NEW EVANGELISM

Consider the evangelism strategy behind the new religion. It has made disciples out of nearly 50 million graduates of colleges and universities over the last decade, while being popularized in arts and entertainment. The new religion teaches its disciples:

- All truth is subjective. (There is no ultimate truth; hence, the Bible and the claims of Christ are irrelevant.

- All sex differences are socially constructed (opening the student up to confusion about gender and experimentation with same sex).

- Western imperialism is the sole source of all third-world problems (fostering contempt for one's nation, ingratitude for the service and sacrifice of others, and disconnection from others who are part of that nation).

- The origins of the United States were evil, including the sins of slavery and the blindness of culture that refuses to see the ongoing inequality caused by systemic white supremacy.

- Religions exist to create a system that reinforces a hierarchy of privilege.

---

8 Hans Von Spakovsky and Charles Stimson, "Teaching Hate Under The Guise Of Inclusion In The US Army." *New York Post*, NYP Holdings, 16 July 2020. https://nypost.com/2020/07/16/teaching-hate-under-the-guise-of-inclusion-in-the-us-army/

- All of life's battles are, in fact, a conflict between competing power groups. The group with more power gets to enjoy the spoils of the conflict and reverse positions with the oppressor.

When spheres of influence like academia, media, entertainment, and politics overlap, they produce a counterfeit of Jesus's command to *"go make disciples of nations."*[9] As students graduate under this indoctrination, they are immediately assimilated into management positions of corporations, finance, media, and entertainment. This army of propagandized youth become the graduates that populate the new workforce in the top of the institutions.

Charlie Kirk says, "What you see on the college campuses, you will soon see on the streets."[10] He was right. Now we see it on our streets.

THE COUNTERFEIT HIERARCHY

Academia, media, and politicians are working synergistically to produce a counterfeit "church leadership" designed to amplify their voice and impact impressionable minds. The New Testament gives us a structure for how the church is supposed to function when Paul taught; *"God has placed in the church first of all apostles, second prophets, third teachers …"* [11]

- Apostles are God's governing leaders.

- Prophets are God's mouthpiece.

- Teachers clarify God's message.

While these first-century church offices are not embraced by all denominations of the twenty-first-century Church, these categories fit into the new fusion of *Progressive Fundamentalism* that forges the mechanism of the counterfeit church.

---

9 Adapted from Matthew 28:19.
10 Charlie Kirk, "Free Speech on College Campuses." National Cable Satellite Convention, 2020. https://www.c-span.org/video/?431563–4/free-speech-college-campuses.
11 1 Corinthians 12:28 (NIV).

In *Progressive Fundamentalism* you have the embodiment of what the New Testament warns of regarding false apostles, false prophets, and false teachers.

False Apostles = Politicians

Paul says false apostles are likened to Satan, who *"disguises himself as an angel of light."*[12] These are the political messiahs who promise utopia in a new political and economic era. The counterfeit apostles are Satan's governing gift.

People who talk about the wars religions have caused ignore the fact that this number is a fraction of the twentieth-century death toll of over 100 million murders under the rise of three socialist/communist political dictators: Hitler, Stalin, and Mau. These three promised utopia but were in reality angels of death. Politics gone bad is far more deadly than religion gone bad. False apostles are made credible because the media goes before them as a mouthpiece, much like John the Baptist paved the way for Jesus.

False Prophets = Media

The false prophets were historically the voices that surrounded a king and spoke to him what the king wanted to hear. True prophets did not do so and were abused by the false prophets. In a scenario such as ours today, the false prophets are the mouthpiece for the politically correct, and everything they say is designed to misrepresent the president and mislead the national audience. They, like the false prophets of old, speak with unity. There is only one entity that fits this description perfectly, and it is labeled "fake news." The modern equivalent of the false prophets is the multiple mouths of the media.

False Teachers = Educators

False teachers have taken over the humanities, social sciences, and classrooms that have educated a new generation of young people to despise

---

12 2 Corinthians 11:14 (NLT).

their nation and identify with the new religious crusade to eradicate "systemic" injustice.

The *Progressive Fundamentalism* religion of today has a counterfeit model in our political leaders as its false apostles, the voice of the media as its false prophets, and academia as its false teachers.

THE FAKE AWAKENING

For years, the left has studied the language of the religious right and co-opted faith terminology to win over evangelicals to their party. It is curious that, at a time when Christians pray for another Great Awakening, the political left counters with their own awakening—getting "woke"—a state of heightened sensitivity to perceived injustice.

> THE PROGRESSIVE FUNDAMENTALISM RELIGION OF TODAY HAS A COUNTERFEIT MODEL IN OUR POLITICAL LEADERS AS ITS FALSE APOSTLES, THE VOICE OF THE MEDIA AS ITS FALSE PROPHETS, AND ACADEMIA AS ITS FALSE TEACHERS.

For this reason, President Obama praised the "Great Awakening" happening around the country. He said, "The good news, what makes me optimistic, is the fact that there is a Great Awakening going on around the country, particularly among younger people who are saying not only are they fed up with the shambolic, disorganized, mean-spirited approach to governance that we've seen over the last couple of years but more than that are eager to take on some of the core challenges that have been facing this country for centuries." [13]

Rather than fostering a sense of personal responsibility, the more "woke" you are, the more you are consciously "awakened" to new levels

---

13 Tal Axelrod, "Obama at Biden fundraiser: 'Whatever You've Done So Far Is
 Not Enough.'" The Hill, 2020.https://thehill.com/homenews/campaign/
 504200-obama-at-biden-fundraiser-whatever-youve-done-so-far-is-not-enough.

of victimhood and oppression. As you can imagine, becoming "woke" is a rather negative experience.

The Achilles heel of this new religion is that it makes everyone miserable. "POP culture is important," as Andrew Breitbart says, "because all politics is downstream from culture."[14] This POP culture is formed by "Pissed Off Progressives." Living in the most prosperous nation with the greatest freedom and opportunity isn't enough. They are angry and rampaging.

Everyone feels the pressure to align with these movements. Who wants to be thought of as a bad person? Who in America is pro-racism? Who in America takes delight in inflicting physical pain on others (other than Antifa, of course.)

Its conversions are forced. People respond, "Yes, of course, I am against racism; I will signal that by promoting your organization." What if you work in a corporation like Amazon, Apple, Nike, or the NFL? You will feel compelled to post your #hashtag in solidarity with your employer. People risk losing their jobs if they don't conform to the counterfeit awakening. You certainly won't exercise your right to post a message explaining concerns. Nobody asks, "Where does my donation go?" What if it goes to a political party?

JUDGMENT DAY

Tuesday, November 3, 2020, will be the most consequential day of your lifetime. November 4 will be more dramatic yet. If the race is tied or if Donald Trump should win, the left will demonstrate its characteristic grace and composure by tearing the nation apart in rage until they have harvested enough votes to keep the revolution going.

However, far more frightening is the idea of Donald Trump losing. The day the new fundamentalists get hold of the presidency, the anarchy will shift, and depending on the condition of Congress and the Senate, varying levels of persecution of the "infidels" will begin.

---

14 Andrew Breitbart, "Politics is Really Downstream from Culture." *Breitbart*, 2020, https://www.breitbart.com/entertainment/2011/08/22/politics-really-is-downstream-from-culture/.

Those who are disloyal to the new deities enshrined in the temple of social justice must be rooted out. Christians who are true to the Bible will be deemed guilty of hate speech. Deplatforming on social media will be the least of your concerns. How bad can it get? Crimes of hate speech will be punishable by various means, not the least of which will be imprisonment, costly fines, seizure of property, and endangerment of family and friends who must socially distance themselves from you and deny all association. After all, they will also come under scrutiny to see if they too are criminals involved in a conspiracy that threatens public safety (also known as a church or home meeting). When the new state religion has sufficient numbers of converts, it will turn the hate speech trial over to citizen tribunals, where the accused can be judged by other citizens deemed loyal.

The main problem that Christians have is that we could never imagine someone doing to us what we would not do to them. David Horowitz, a former leftist turned whistleblower, puts it all in clear perspective: "The chief strategy of Democratic political campaigns is the politics of personal destruction. Any strategy for resisting these attacks has to begin with an understanding of this brutal fact." Horowitz says, "The first requirement for any strategy to stop their progressive agenda is to understand that they have tremendous hatred in their hearts for those who oppose them."[15] They are not neutral. They do not separate the person from the opinion. They link the two together. Where Christians might say they separate the sin from the sinner, the left would say the two are actually one—and the sinner is you.

Horowitz continues:

> The second requirement is to know how to confound that hatred. If your opponents are prepared to demonize you as a racist and you have no equally powerful response you might as well quit the field of battle. [Or wait till they kick you out.] Why do progressives have hatred in their hearts for Conservatives? Why do they sound like hellfire-and-damnation preachers when they are on the attack? Because they are zealots of what can only be described as a crypto-religion [crypto meaning a secret allegiance to a

---

15 David Horowitz. *BIG AGENDA: President Trump's Plan to Save America.* (Humanix, 2017).

creed] modeled on the Christian narrative of the fall and redemption—the difference being that they see themselves as the redeemers instead of the divinity. To progressives, the world is a fallen place—beset by racism, sexism, homophobia, and the rest—that must be transformed and made right.[16]

The redemption they advocate for was once called "communism" but is now branded as "socialism," working through it's more popular and deceptive guise of "social justice." They share a counterfeit kingdom vision of a utopian world of politically enforced equality. They seek a geo-political one-world safe place where there are no politically incorrect deplorables. Christianity and all such irredeemables must be assimilated into the new order or outlawed and governmentally suppressed.

Progressives believe that politically enforced equality is achievable by taxing the rich until there are no more poor. No borders. No nations. No police. No armies. Progressives are enthralled by their dreams of a heaven on earth. What decent soul would be against a world where everyone was guaranteed a living wage, healthcare, a free education, with no fossil fuels and social justice in a unified world without borders? Progressives are social redeemers—without the gospel of Jesus or the anointing. They seek the millennium rule of Christ without Christ. Consequently, they regard themselves as the army of the saints and those who oppose them as the party of the damned, whose selfishness must be eradicated. It is not hard to imagine that in such a world, those who kill you *will think they are doing God a service.*[17] Of course, the glaring Achilles heel at the heart of all this is the raging naivety that the Chinese Communist Party and revived Caliphates will cheerfully pull up a chair in the midst of the collapsed rubble of the West and join the American progressives vision.

THE ULTIMATE FIREWALL

If everyone else collapses in the face of social pressure, the Christian has no choice but to stand in humble defiance. They cannot be compelled to recant truth simply because someone is telling them what they believe is not

---

16 David Horowitz. *BIG AGENDA: President Trump's Plan to Save America.* (Humanix, 2017).

17 Adapted from John 16:2 (Berean Study Bible).

acceptable. The sixteenth-century reformer Martin Luther went on trial for his life over his unwavering commitment to scripture and conscience. "Unless I am convinced by Scripture and plain reason—I do not accept the authority of the popes and councils, for they have contradicted each other—my conscience is captive to the Word of God. I cannot and I will not recant anything, for to go against conscience is neither right nor safe. God help me. Amen." [18] His unwillingness to back down in the face of martyrdom produced shockwaves that changed the world. The Reformation he catalyzed forged the foundation beneath Western Civilization and the liberties beneath the Bill of Rights. The Reformation was a blow to the entire culture of hierarchy in Europe, equalizing all mankind, teaching that in Christ there is no longer a division between priest and man. Luther's *priesthood of all believers*, laid the foundation for another writer to say "all men are created equal."

Luther's bold stand modeled that individuals before God have a right to think and worship and speak the truth, even when they are in the minority. The Reformation sets the sovereignty of man against the dictates of kings, popes, and the tyranny of the 51 percent, where the majority rules. That fundamental idea of a sovereign man speaking the truth in the face of the collective, majority, or government is the basis of religious freedom—that this right is given by God and not the state, which is evidenced as the opening premise of the Declaration of Independence.

Modern day reformers like Martin Luther are facing off with the tyranny of man once again, and our only answer to a militant paganism is a militant church. The question is, what does that look like? Having already ceded ground in academia, entertainment, media, corporations, and small business, the last line of defense will be pastors and ministers. Even now, they are being forced to draw a line between submission to government and violation of conscience.

What is a militant church called to do? One of the most significant passages in the Old Testament is Jeremiah 1:9–10. The young prophet was told "*to root out and to pull down, to destroy and to throw down, to build and to*

---

18 Martin Luther, "Luther at the Imperial Diet of Worms." 16 Apr 1521, https://www.luther.de/en/worms.html.

plant."[19] Four out of six of these words describe the dismantling of strongholds that must precede building and planting.

Over the last few decades, while the church was at peace, it could retreat from defeats in the culture wars and focus inward on "building and planting" its own vision. Now the battle lines are being redrawn. In order to build, we must survive; and to survive, we must fight in a different way. If all politics is downstream from culture and you want to change the culture, you will have to move upstream and interrupt the narrative. You have to challenge it and articulate a disruptive, compelling, better story. You have to stop hiding from the media and run to the fire. You have to be willing to be ridiculed and mocked if in exchange you can score points with those who are persuadable.

Since the coronavirus pandemic began, when governors of states began telling Christians they can only meet when the government permits, a boundary was crossed for many Christians. When the government said you cannot meet in homes to sing or worship with a small group, an alarm went off in the hearts of many believers. The targeted persecution was only made more evident when those same governors allowed protestors to gather in the street for weeks.

The "silent majority" is becoming silent no more in the face of a *Progressive Fundamentalism* that cannot coexist with traditional America. Within the silent majority are twenty-five million people who are spiritually active and who watch the government and observe media manipulation like a hawk. These people are SAGECons—spiritually active and governmentality engaged conservatives—who make up a bulk of the conservative radio audience and who can be easily mobilized. In addition to this group there are thirty million Christians who *do not vote* but who make up a sizable part of the middle class that will reassert themselves when their values are under siege. They are just now waking up to the realization that America has been hijacked. How do you think they are going to respond?

---

19 Jeremiah 1:10 (NKJV).

LET'S ROLL!

On the morning of September 11, 2001, Al Qaeda committed one of the deadliest terrorist attacks in US history by hijacking four commercial airliners and using them as weapons.

Thirty-three passengers and seven crew members were aboard United Airlines Flight 93, en route from Newark, New Jersey, to San Francisco, California. Among the passengers were four hijackers who had hidden knives and box cutters in their carry-on luggage. At 9:32 a.m., according to the flight data recorder, a man later identified as Ziad Jarrah told the passengers there was a bomb on board. Jarrah, who was a trained pilot, directed them to move to the back of the plane, sit down, and be quiet. He then disabled the autopilot and turned the plane back east.

The crew and passengers huddled in the back of the plane and called family members and officials on the ground, telling them their flight had been hijacked. They quickly realized their plane was being used to carry out another attack on a US target after learning of the three other hijacked flights in New York City and Washington, DC. Realizing they had to do something, the passengers and cabin crew took a quick vote and made their decision.

Thomas Burnett Jr., one of the passengers, told his wife over the phone, "I know we're all going to die. There's three of us who are going to do something about it. I love you, honey." [1] One of those three passengers, Todd Beamer, had tried to place a call to his family but was routed to airphone supervisor Lisa Jefferson. Beamer told Jefferson that hijackers had taken control of United Flight 93, that two of the hijackers had knives, and that one appeared to have a bomb strapped to him. Beamer recited the Lord's Prayer and the Twenty-Third Psalm with Jefferson, prompting others to join in. Then he made a request of Jefferson: "If I don't make it, please call my family and let them know how much I love them." After this, Jefferson could not make out what was said but recalled muffled voices; then she clearly heard Beamer saying, "Are you ready? Okay. Let's roll."[20] These would be Beamer's last known words.

---

20 Flight 93." *History.com*, A&E Television Networks LLC, 2020, https://www. history.com/.amp/topics/21st-century/flight-93.

At 9:57 a.m., the three passengers rushed down the aisle and launched their unexpected counterattack. The plane's controls were turned hard to the right, and amidst muffled voices and shouts the plane descended rapidly and exploded in an empty field in Shanksville, Pennsylvania. It is believed that the passengers of United 93 saved the White House that day.

Now we face a new religion that has captured the minds of radicals who have stormed the "cockpit," and once again, we risk losing the White House. It's time to take back America.

CHAPTER 8

THE STORM IS HERE

"In order to realize the worth of the anchor
we need to feel the stress of the storm."
—*Corrie Ten Boom*

We are facing a different kind of American storm, an ideologic storm empowered by hell and intent on redefining who we are as a nation. Our internal divisions are increasingly fed and inflamed by foreign governments, such as the EU, globalists, and China. Under the clever disguise of noble-sounding causes, well-funded activist organizations spread confusion and feed societal fragmentation as they lay siege to our minds, our cities, and our nation's soul. They will not stop until all the political and judicial levers of power are in their hands. For more reasons than COVID, the nation is dealing with an "invisible enemy." If we do nothing to stop this demonic turbulence, it will not simply go away, *it will actually increase and intensify.* America in November 2020 is the flood barrier wall upon which this storm now breaks. It has been like watching a tropical storm ramp up into a category 5 hurricane, and now as the eye of the storm is about to make landfall, the question on everyone's mind is, "Will the ship of state be able weather the storm or will it sink?" As it intensifies, we must learn to deal with the organizational structures looking to exploit the turbulence and the spirits working behind them.

When it comes to spiritual warfare, the battle is never against flesh and blood, but against unseen "principalities and powers" that occupy "heavenly places."[1] Jesus, in all things, is our model; and He dispossessed demons in people, places, and territories.

In Mark 4:35, we find one of the most powerful accounts of Jesus dealing with the invisible realm. After preaching to the multitudes, when evening came, Jesus instructed his disciples to dismiss the crowd and to *"cross to the other side"*[2] of the Sea of Galilee. Jesus, weary from the day, found a place in the hull of the boat to sleep as they sailed.

That evening, a ferocious storm overtook the boat as strong winds tossed them to and fro. The storm raged, but Jesus remained asleep. Four of the disciples on board the boat were experienced fishermen; yet the disciples panicked and woke Jesus shouting, *"Teacher, don't you care that we're going to drown!?"*[3] Jesus, once awake, assessed the situation, stepped forward, and rebuked the wind and the waves: *"Peace! Be still!"* The storm subsided, the winds ceased, and a great calm enveloped the waters. His disciples were astonished.

The Greek word for **"be still"** *(phimoó)*[4] literally means, "to be muzzled." Jesus uses the same word in Mark 1:25 after a demon-possessed man approached him in the temple and cried out, *"What do you want with us, Jesus of Nazareth? Have you come to destroy us? I know who you are—the Holy One of God!"* Jesus sternly rebuked the demon, and said *"**Be quiet** (phimoó)! Come out of him!"* [5] Since this is the same word Jesus used when rebuking the storm, this tells us that the Galilee squall was no normal storm; there was a spiritual intelligence behind it.

When Jesus arrived in Gadarenes on the other side of the lake, *"There met him out of the city a certain man, who had devils for a long time, and wore no clothes, neither abode in any house, but in the tombs."* [6] This tormented man was fierce, having broken every chain used to restrain him. He was like a half human, howling at night and cutting himself with stones. The moment Jesus arrived, the demon-possessed man was drawn to Jesus, and the demons cried out, *"What have I to do with you, Jesus, Son of God most*

---

1 Adapted from Ephesians 6:12.
2 Mark 4:35 (ESV).
3 Mark 4:38 (NLT).
4 BibleHub s.v. "phimoo" (v), https://biblehub.com/greek/5392.htm.
5 Mark 1:24–25 (NIV).
6 Luke 8:27 (King James 2000 Bible).

high? I beg you, torment me not."[7] Amazingly, the devils knew the true identity of Jesus, even when no one else did. In contrast, the storm came in order to stop Jesus from entering new territory on the other side of Galilee, the demonized man was not coming to attack—the storm inside of him was seeking resolution. He wanted freedom, and Jesus would give it to him. When the strongman behind the storm was rebuked, deliverance of the captive on the ground was made possible.

Mark states that the demons *"besought him much that he would not **send them away out of the country.**"*[8] Jesus gave them permission to enter a herd of swine; but after the demons entered, the herd raced over a cliff and drowned in the water below. The man's deliverance was so dramatic that the entire city came out to see for themselves the once-demonized man clothed and in his right mind conversing with Jesus.

SEEING THE UNSEEN

At first glance, it doesn't seem like these two stories are connected, but *the storm and the demoniac are linked!* There were two levels of spiritual activity—a higher level in the atmosphere operating over the territory and another lower level that took up residence inside a person under its jurisdiction. The territorial strongman at work behind the storm tried to drown Jesus and His disciples on the way to Gadarenes. When Jesus delivered the Gadarene, the disembodied spirits were sent into a herd of pigs and driven over a cliff into the sea. The drowning was reversed.

The reason the spirit storm showed up was because Jesus was invading its territory. As He got closer in proximity, the storm intensified in order to resist him. We know in hindsight that Jesus was going into new geography where a major spiritual stronghold was about to come down. The moment Jesus arrived, the most demonized man in the region found Christ. We do not know why, but it seems that the desperation of his human condition was drawn to the living God.

Like a moth drawn to a flame, wherever Jesus went, the spirit realm knew He was there and could not suppress itself from manifesting in His

7 Luke 8:28 (King James 2000 Bible).
8 Mark 5:10 (KJV).

presence. Notice when these Gadarene spirits spoke to Jesus, they made it clear they did not want to leave the area—they were territorial. When you are called as a change agent, you will attract both divine appointments and spirits that operate in that territory.

Christians are by nature missionaries. There are times when you are sent into an unfamiliar environment and sense something that you could not know in the natural. You may be sensing a dark, oppressive atmosphere over a city or an organization, or even a spiritual attack targeting someone you are called to meet or minister to in that new environment.

I once heard a preacher say, "God is a territorial Spirit." It sounded odd to me until he explained what he meant: God had moved from a physical temple in the Old Covenant to the temple of His people, the body of Christ, in the New Covenant. As a believer the Holy Spirit dwells inside you. Paul likened himself to being an ambassador. Every ambassador has an embassy. The embassy is ground governed by the laws of the nation the ambassador represents. When God sends you somewhere, you are bringing the embassy with you.

LIVE, NATION SACRED IN GOD, DON'T DIE!

I was speaking in Prague when one of my team members experienced this embassy phenomenon. I had just flown in, along with my son Carl, who joined in the lectures, and Mercedes Sparks, my VP of Operations. Upon arrival, Mercedes was overwhelmed with uncharacteristic heaviness and thoughts of suicide for two days. She sought the Lord about what was happening because this was not her unusual disposition. The Lord instructed her to make a declaration over the city seven times, "Prague, you shall live and not die." She obeyed, and after that time of intercession, the heaviness broke and the suicidal thoughts departed. She was back to normal. She looked up the history of Prague and discovered that the country had passed through Nazi occupation and violent Stalinist suppression. Today, thankfully, it is a city where Christians are free to speak.

The next day, our hosts took us on a tour of the city. In the public square, we came upon a statue dedicated to the martyr Jan Hus. Hus was a reformer who spoke out against the Catholic Church's selling of indulgences and the moral failings of its clergy. For his outspoken stance, Hus was arrested, tried, and told to recant. He declared that he was willing to recant *if* someone could prove from the Bible that his teachings were in error. No such argument was available, and Hus was condemned to death as a heretic against the doctrines of the Catholic Church. Hus was taken to the cathedral, dressed in his priestly garments, then stripped of them one by one. At the stake, he refused to recant for the last time. He prayed, *"Lord Jesus, it is for thee that I patiently endure this cruel death. I pray thee to have mercy on my enemies."*[9]

As flames engulfed him, he was heard reciting the Psalms. Hus was martyred on July 6, 1415. We noticed the date when we stood there looking at the monument. In less than 24 hours, it would be July 6, 2018, exactly 303 years to the day Hus died.

That bold martyr sustains his influence in Prague to this day. After his death, the people of Bohemia moved even further away from papal teachings. A century after his death, as many as ninety percent of inhabitants of the Czech lands were non-Catholic; to this day some still follow the teachings of Hus. The Czech's formed a political and military response to Rome called Hussites. They were forerunners of the Protestant Reformation that would take hold a hundred years later. By asserting their independence from Rome, the Hussite movement represented an early expression of Czech nationalism.

The grand statue of Jan Hus in the city square. As we approached the statue, the tour guide explained, "And here is a statue of Jan Hus inscribed on one side with the words 'Live, Nation Sacred in God; Don't Die.'"[10] This was the *exact* proclamation the Lord had given to Mercedes when she was interceding for the destiny of the nation!

When Mercedes entered the territory in Prague, she sensed a spirit of death and despair. As the spiritual storm surrounded her, God instructed her to speak to the storm and intercede for the nation. Know that if God gives you the ability to sense or discern something, it is not about you; it is about the assignment you carry for that territory.

---

9 Special To People's World, "Today In History: Jan Hus Burned At The Stake 600 Years Ago." People's World, 6 July 2015. https://www.peoplesworld.org/article/today-in-history-jan-hus-burned-at-the-stake-600-years-ago/

10 "Jan Hus Monument In The Middle Of The Old Town Square." Prague.cz, Martin Muller, 2011. http://prague.cz/jan-hus-monument/

(Jan Hus Monument, "Live, Nation Sacred in God; Don't Die," Erected in 1915)

BREAKING DEMONIC
SPELLS OVER AMERICA

Now consider the chaos erupting in American cities where our greatest national troubles exist. The current labels of Red State and Blue State is an increasing indicator of what kind of spiritual environment dominates the atmosphere. Individual states actually become regional sheep- and goat-oriented environments. The Bible uses the word *thrones* to describe the invisible realm that operates over physical territory. Again, let's look at what Paul wrote to the church in Colossae: *"For in Him all things were created, things in heaven and on earth, **visible and invisible**, whether thrones or dominions or rulers or authorities. All things were created through Him and for Him. He is before all things, and in Him all things hold together."*[11]

Paul is saying there are invisible thrones and visible thrones, and there are invisible rulers and visible rulers. Is it not possible that invisible thrones refer to a seat of a ruling spirit over a territory? The fact that these thrones are referred to in the Bible is most interesting. What empowers or challenges these thrones? It seems likely that the spiritual climate of a city is

---

11 Colossians 1:16–17 (NIV).

connected to the people living in that environment, and the church can play a vital role in shaping that atmosphere.

Have you ever walked into a room where people were talking negatively about you before you arrived? Can you recall what it felt like? Or have you ever showed up at a place where everyone was looking forward to your arrival? What was it like? In both cases, we are talking about something called the power of agreement, which can be positive or negative. The principle of agreement is fundamental to how prayer operates. Even when non-Christians come together in one mind and agree with an ungodly belief, they actually empower that ungodly belief to become manifest to various degrees. That is why there are geographic hot spots of rage and destruction that are linked to the invisible realm we've been describing. This is even more pronounced when there is widespread humility and unity in the Body of Christ. When the people of God come into agreement, they have authority in the territory to challenge the gates of hell and see some measure of healing and revival spring forth.

In reality, what Christians call "spiritual warfare" is more than just spiritual; it's the collusion of spirits *and* human organizations that have the power to either heal and reconcile or divide and conquer the nation by stirring hatred between genders, races, and social economic classes.

I believe that riots and civil unrest in cities are connected by a threefold cord joining the vulnerabilities of people, the agenda of political/social organizations operating in cities, and the territorial spirits that dominate a geography. As activists come into a territory, they activate the people and stir up the territorial spirits to mobilize manifestation.

For example, in the book of Acts, spiritually charged protests took place in various cities such as Ephesus after Paul entered the territory:

About that time there arose a great disturbance about the Way. A silversmith named Demetrius, who made silver shrines of Artemis, brought in a lot of business for the craftsmen there. He called them together, along with the workers in related trades, and said: 'You know, my friends, that we receive a good income from this business. And you see and hear how this fellow Paul has convinced and led astray large numbers of people here in Ephesus and in practically the whole province of Asia. He says that gods made by human hands are no gods at all. There is danger not only that our trade will lose its good name, but also that the temple of the great goddess Artemis will be discredited; and the goddess herself, who is worshiped throughout the province of Asia and the world, will be robbed of her divine majesty.'

Paul's message was a disruption to the financial interests of powerful people.

When they heard this, they were furious and began shouting: 'Great is Artemis of the Ephesians!' Soon the whole city was in an uproar. The people seized Gaius and Aristarchus, Paul's traveling companions from Macedonia, and all of them rushed into the theater together. Paul wanted to appear before the crowd, but the disciples would not let him. Even some of the officials of the province, friends of Paul, sent him a message begging him not to venture into the theater.

The devil was stirring up Demetrius and his trade alliance to create a social disruption in order to stop the influence of Paul's message. Spiritual turbulence produced a chaos that sucked people into its vortex. Many did not even know what they were protesting.

The assembly was in confusion: Some were shouting one thing, some another. Most of the people did not even know why they were there. *The Jews in the crowd pushed Alexander to the front, and they shouted instructions to him. He motioned for silence in order to make a defense before the people. But* **when they realized he was a Jew, they all shouted in unison for about two hours: "Great is Artemis of the Ephesians!"**

The city clerk quieted the crowd *and said: "Fellow Ephesians, doesn't all the world know that the city of Ephesus is the guardian of the temple of the great Artemis and of her image, which fell from heaven? Therefore, since these facts are undeniable, you ought to calm down and not do anything rash. You have brought these men here, though they have neither robbed temples nor blasphemed our goddess. If, then, Demetrius and his fellow craftsmen have a grievance against anybody, the courts are open and there are proconsuls. They can press charges. If there is anything further you want to bring up, it must be settled in a legal assembly.* **As it is, we are in danger of being charged with rioting because of what happened today. In that case we would not be able to account for this commotion, since there is no reason for it."** *After he had said this, he dismissed the assembly.[12]*

12 Acts 19:23–41 (NIV).

In every city, no matter the century, there will be vested interests, which are threatened by movements that persuade the masses. Add the Gospel, and it's like kerosine on the fire. In the city of Ephesus we see how the devil was working through *"Demetrius and his fellow craftsmen."*[13] The city's ruling elites were threatened, so they decided to provoke the city to a riot to get rid of the messenger exposing their racket. For two hours, they chanted the same slogan until a city official stepped in to calm the crowd and remind them of the need for law and order, at which point they finally dispersed.

This verse reads like it was taken from today's headlines. While the George Floyd protests in Minneapolis started off peacefully, they veered off course and turned into violent riots, destroying businesses and communities after they were taken over by organizations like Antifa and Black Lives Matters (BLM). Two organizations like *"Demetrius and his fellow craftsmen"* with their own agendas, intent on escalating protest into a cultural, political, and even spiritual *revolution*.

WHAT YOU BOW TO ON THE WAY UP CONTROLS YOU AT THE TOP

I started tracking BLM a few years ago when I heard that George Soros[14] was funding the organization. Recently BLM has risen to the forefront to become a 2.5-billion-dollar corporately funded organization, thanks to sponsors like the NBA, NFL, EA Games, Ubisoft, ETSY, H&M, and so many more. Virtually all major retailers have financially contributed to BLM, yet almost no one knows what this organization *actually* supports.[15]

---

13 Acts 19:38 (NIV).
14 "George Soros Gave Black Lives Matter And Antifa Over 100 Million Dollars." *News Break,* Particle Media, 2013. https://www.newsbreak.com/district-of-columbia/washington/news/1583520112758/george-soros-gave-black-lives-matter-and-antifa-over-100-million-dollars1583520112758/george-soros-gave-black-lives-matter-and-antifa-over-100-million-dollars
15 Mercey Livingston, "These Are Major Brands Donating To Black Lives Matter." CNet, 16 June 2020. https://www.cnet.com/how-to/companies-donating-black-lives-matter/

BLM co-founder Patrisse Cullors does not hide the fact that she is a "trained Marxist."[16] The BLM's website under "What We Believe,"[17] keeps changing to accommodate public scrutiny. The current site has wiped away what they really believe. For years things like disrupting "the Western-prescribed nuclear family structure" or doing the "work required to dismantle cisgender privilege and uplift Black trans folk" was front and center on their website. These are the BLM issues the NFL and all these other corporations want to support. If this doesn't confuse you, you're not paying attention.

You may be asking yourself, what is "cisgender privilege?" The prefix "cis" means "on the same side as." So if you were identified at birth as a boy or girl, or male or female and you stay with that, you are part of the "cisgender privilege." Let's also define transgender: this is someone who does not identify with the body they were given at birth. If you are born with the physical characteristics of a biological boy but think you are a girl, you have a clash between biology and psychology. The traditional approach would be to work to bring peace and healing by reconciling the person back into their biological gender. The transgender movement insists the order be reversed so that psychology trumps biology.

Finally what is a "nuclear family"? It is a family consisting of a married man and woman with children. This, according to BLM, needs to be "disrupted." They want to do this in spite of the fact that children born into a stable marriage tend to be better off than children born into cohabitation. Pew Research Center found that *20 percent of kids born to married parents* experience divorce, while nearly *50 percent of kids in cohabiting families* experience divorce. Both of these groups of children have a better chance to one day live with a married couple than kids born to single moms.[18]

---

16 Freedom Forum, "BLM Cofounder Admits; We Are Trained Marxists." *YouTube Video,* 1:09. July 2, 2020. https://www.youtube.com/watch?v=p7C6tNjiRKY

17 Joshua Rhett Miller, BLM Removes Website on Nuclear Family Structure Amid NFL Vets Criticism." *New York Post.* New York Post Holdings LLC, 2020. https://nypost.com/2020/09/24/blm-removes-website-language-blasting-nuclear-family-structure/

18 Michele Meelin, "Pros and Cons of the Nuclear Family." LovetoKnow, 2020. https://family.lovetoknow.com/advantages-disadvantages-nuclear-family

Do we *really* want to disrupt families? The argument for building stronger heterosexual marriages makes sense as a child benefits from a male and female in different ways, but regardless, why disrupt this? Why attack the mom-and-dad model? Why attack men in particular? Do single-parent homes need an extended network of support? Yes. When you hear "it takes a village" to raise a child, a healthy church is that village, and in it you know who and what is influencing your child. What would 2.5 billion dollars do for cities if these churches were funded to reach single moms and children thirteen and under? In one decade, there would be a statistical impact.

What is even more alarming isn't even the agenda but the potential spiritual motivations driving it. During a program hosted by the Fowler Museum at UCLA, Cullors and Melina Abdullah, co-founders of Black Lives Matter–Los Angeles, discussed the role that spirituality has played in the Black Lives Matter movement. In the interview, Abdullah said it took her almost a year before she realized Black Lives Matter was much more than a racial and social justice movement. "At its core, it's a spiritual movement," she said.[19] Cullors, in startling detail, revealed the extent to which they are tapping into the spirit realm when calling out the names of the victims. "It is literally almost resurrecting a spirit so they can work through us to get the work that we need to get done."[20] Abdullah added that, "We become very intimate with the spirits that we call on regularly. Right, like, each of them seems to have a different presence and personality. You know, I laugh a lot with Wakisha [sic], you know, and I didn't meet her in her body. Right, I met her through this work."[21] Wakiesha Wilson was an African American woman found dead in a Los Angeles jail

19 Alejandra Molina, "Black Lives Matter Is A Spiritual Movement." Religion News Service, 15 June 2020. https://religionnews.com/2020/06/15/why-black-lives-matter-is-a-spiritual-movement-says-blm-co-founder-patrisse-cullors/

20 Alejandra Molina, "Black Lives Matter Is A Spiritual Movement." June 15, 2020. https://religionnews.com/2020/06/15/why-black-lives-matter-is-a-spiritual-movement-says-blm-co-founder-patrisse-cullors/

21 Michael Brown. "Are BLM Leaders Calling on the Spirits of the Dead?" Living Faith Christian Forums and Discussion. Aug 2015. https://livingfaithforum.com/discussing-politics/8961-blm-leaders-calling-spirits-dead.html

in 2016. These are more than slogans; they are an appeal to the spirits of the deceased to rise up and work through her and others.

At a protest on June 2, 2020, in front of LA Mayor Eric Garcetti's home, Abdullah was reported to have led a group of demonstrators in a ritual. As part of the ceremony, people recited the names of "those taken by state violence before their time," calling them back to animate their own justice. After calling on each name, Abdullah poured libations on the ground as the group of 100 in return chanted "Asé."[22] Hebah Farrag, in a blog titled "The Fight for Black Lives is a Spiritual Movement," explained that "Asé" "is a Yoruba term often used by practitioners of Ifa, a faith and divination system that originated in West Africa." "This ritual," Dr. Abdullah explained, "is a form of worship."[23]

The person who first exposed the spiritual roots of BLM and linked it to witchcraft was Abraham Hamilton III in his August 19, 2020, podcast, *The BLM Connection to Witchcraft*.[24] Hamilton is the public policy analyst for the American Family Association and holds a Juris Doctor degree from Loyola University, New Orleans College of Law. In his podcast, Hamilton criticized the Black Lives Matter movement as a "Marxist, anti-Christ, anti-family, [and] anti-man organization."[25] He goes on to say that BLM is a, "copy and paste of the Bolshevik Revolution ... just applied to an American context." Hamilton ended his broadcast by challenging his audience, "How can you reconcile that with what the Word of God says? ... We have got [sic] to evaluate everything through the word of God." If the BLM movement is actually rooted in spiritual activity, Christians who support it should understand what they are endorsing.

---

22 Hebah Farrag, "The Fight For Black Lives Is A Spiritual Movement." Berkley Center, 9 June 2020. https://berkleycenter.georgetown.edu/responses/the-fight-for-black-lives-is-a-spiritual-movement

23 Ibid.

24 The Hamilton Corner With Abraham Hamilton, "The BLM Connection To Witchcraft." Facebook, 2020. https://www.facebook.com/watch/?v=313241209918422&extid=24VzdkXvzgwT29CT

25 Derek Kim, "Podcast Host Abraham Hamilton Accuses Black Lives Matter Leaders Of Practicing Witchcraft." Christianity Daily, 4 Sept 2020. http://www.christianitydaily.com/articles/9818/20200904/podcast-host-abraham-hamilton-accuses-black-lives-matter-leaders-of-practicing-witchcraft.htm

Shelby Steele, an African-American veteran of the civil rights movement of the 1960s and a best-selling author, was on with Mark Levin on Fox News and spoke to the heart of what is driving protests. He gave his observation of the 2020 riots saying this:

"What do they want? I remember growing up in the civil rights movement, everybody knew exactly what we wanted … This insurrection just seems just sort of unclear. It's unmotivated by anything it says itself.

So what is it really about? I think what is really happening is that there is nothing really new. The civil rights argument that triggered this, that there was police abuse, is a very familiar story. We saw that in Ferguson, Missouri.

It seems to me that in many ways it's about power. In order to pursue power as they do, you have to have victims… Wow, the excitement that creates on the Left. It validates their claims that America is a wretched country. They must get their recourse…" He goes on to discuss the thinking behind those in movement, *"Society is responsible for us, because racism is so systemic"* He concludes, *"Well, that's a corruption, and I know it's a corruption, because the truth of the matter is blacks have never been less oppressed than they are today. Opportunity is around every corner. In all of this, no one ever stops to say, 'well, you are unhappy with where minorities are at in American life'… well why don't you take some responsibility for it?"*[26]

LIFE AND LIBERTY

One faith-filled activist who has already stepped into this vacuum is Bob Woodson, founder and president of the Woodson Center. He is an American community-development leader who identifies grassroots "Josephs" all over the country, who are changing communities in high-crime, low-income neighborhoods. He calls them Josephs because, like the biblical character Joseph, they overcome adversity and captivity to deliver their people. These men and women are transforming their communities. Woodson explains, "Once we find solutions that are developed by the people suffering the problem, we provide training, we provide them access

---

26 Shelby Steele joins 'Life, Liberty & Levin.' 6 Jun 2020. https://video.foxnews.com/ v/6162032365001#sp=show-clips

to money, and then we determine, what are the policy barriers that prevent them from maximizing? ... So if someone is successfully reaching 50 kids in the community and reducing their violent behavior, we provide them with the assistance they need so they can grow, so they're affecting 500 kids."[27] Woodson's grassroots leaders have trained 2,500 people in thirty-eight states, all from different racial and ethnic groups.

Spiritual work is practical work, and the real systemic problem isn't racism, it's greed. Woodson says, "In 1960, when the government started spending $22 trillion, 70 cents of every dollar did not go to the poor, it went to those who served the poor. **They asked not which problems are solvable, but which ones are fundable. And so what happened is we've created a commodity out of poor people.** And so, as a consequence, there was (sic) no incentives to solve problems of the poor because the careers of those serving them were dependent upon having people to serve.... Up until 1960, eighty-five percent of all black families had a man and a woman raising children."[28] That figure is now reversed; 75 percent of all African American families today are single-parent households. "So social policies of the '60s did what racism couldn't have accomplished before. And that's why in the black community, you've seen the families disintegrate over the last 50 years, when prior – but a hundred years prior to that, black families were intact."[29]

The families that need the most support are led by single black mothers. A few years ago, my wife discovered that the DFW Metroplex has one of the highest homeless single-mother family populations in the nation. I remember the day my beautiful wife of thirty-five years, Annabelle, came home and told me she just found out that mothers were living in cars with their children in Fort Worth, Texas, and she was going to do something about it. That is when she launched Furnishing Families of Texas, the outreach arm of Lance Wallnau Ministries.

---

27 "Bob Woodson On Supporting High Achieving Families In Low Income Communities, Countering New York Times 1916 Project." *Fox News,* 2020. https://www.foxnews.com/transcript/bob-woodson-on-supporting-high-achieving-families-in-low-income-communities-countering-ny-times-1619-project

28 Ibid.

29 Ibid.

We had a water disaster in our home and needed to give away a bedroom set. She called a local charity; and within minutes, they gave her the name and number of a woman who just moved from a shelter to an apartment and needed a queen bed . The woman asked if she could also get a twin bed for her seven-year-old son and said that he had never slept in a bed in his life. He had slept on a couch, in a car, and on an air mattress but not on a bed.

Annabelle told her close friend Wanda about the conversation, and Wanda responded, "Not on my watch!" and then proceeded to buy the first twin bed they ever gave away. A year later, the mom called to tell her that the bed was a game changer for her son. In fact he became top math student in the whole third grade of his school. His mom was positive that it was because he had a good night sleep every night that his scholastic performance increased.

Up until that time that young seven-year-old was like hundreds of children who sleep without a bed, going through the motions every day without extra stamina and focus. I'm talking about the fact that this is happening in zip codes one or two numbers different than ours.

Now that Furnishing Families of Texas has been launched, she hears about and responds to more and more families all the time. The ministry doesn't advertise to get clients. It works by word of mouth. So far they've given away over 150 beds, bedding, tables, couches, and housewares for single moms in just two years.

She's had to rent one, two, and now three warehouses to meet the needs of these families. She started paying for Uber to pick up her newly adopted spiritual daughters so those who needed rides to their jobs could get to work. In addition, she started asking God to send her cars, and the first one was recently donated and given to a family in need. This outreach isn't in Mozambique; it's here in America, less than twenty minutes from our home in the DFW Metroplex. No longer can we live spiritually isolated lives apart from the need that is calling us.

People like Bob Woodson and Annabelle Wallnau are part of the Great American Awakening. Like Bob and Annabelle, don't hide yourself from the need that is calling you. Quite often the call of God comes in the form of a problem. To identify their calling, many seek to discover their passion. Your passion may not be a pleasure you pursue; it may be a problem you are anointed to solve. One man suggested you ask yourself, "What problem keeps you up at night? What is it that makes you weep or want to pound the table?" When the apostle Paul made two unsuccessful attempts to get into territory he thought he was supposed to go into, the Lord gave him a vision of a man in Philippi crying out, "Help us!" The next day, he was off on one of the greatest adventures of his life.

The American storm is larger than racial, gender, and political division. When the disciples feared that the storm would sink the boat, they cried out and awakened Jesus who arose to rebuke the storm. The challenge for us is that there is no physical Jesus to awaken—**it is the sleeping body of Christ that must awaken and speak to the storm**. Angry waves have overtaken the ship, and demonic winds may lash the vessel violently, but God is on board this boat. To quell the ferocity of the storm, it's going to take all of us finding our place in the midst of the crisis, the chaos, and the call of God.

CHAPTER 9

THE DAY CHRISTIANS
CHANGED HISTORY

"Democracy is two wolves and a lamb voting on what to have for lunch. Liberty is a well-armed Lamb contesting the vote."[1]
—*Benjamin Franklin*

In 2015, Christians looked with dread at the prospect of being governed as despised "deplorables" under Hillary Clinton. Over the course of the primaries they rallied behind one Christian political savior after another. All good men, but God had prepared an unlikely deliverer. God was doing a new thing. Donald Trump would become the modern-day Cyrus ruler America needed.

At the time, only 25 percent of evangelicals were enthusiastic. This was until a turning point happened at a meeting in New York City at the Marriott Hotel, sponsored by Ken Eldred and United in Purpose. What was supposed to be a meeting with 300 key evangelicals swelled to a meeting with over a thousand. Free from the filter of biased media, Donald Trump could speak candidly about who he was and what he believed needed to happen in America. The results were electric. Doubters became believers—his approval with evangelicals shot up from 25 percent to over 85 percent, and we have never looked back.

---

1 "Benjamin Franklin On Liberty." Mises Institute, 2 Feb 2003. https://mises.org/library/ben-franklin-liberty

Going into election night, Donald Trump was trailing Hillary Clinton by five points in some polls and by ten points in other polls. Franklin Graham texted Mike Pence that a victory for the Trump campaign would be nothing less than a miracle. That night, we all got our miracle.

The election came down to four swing states and a margin of about 241,000 votes out of some 138 million votes cast nationwide. Consider how razor thin that margin in victory was: Wisconsin (27,257 votes), Michigan (13,080 votes), Pennsylvania (68,236 votes), and Florida (114,455 votes). [2] In 2016 it was the Church that showed up as the swing-state remnant vote that put Trump over the top and into office. We were an undocumented group no pollsters had on their radar, yet we are comprised of twenty-two million Americans. In 2016 it was George Barna who coined the name "SAGECons" (spiritually active, governmentally engaged conservatives) for this group.

Leading into election day, an uneasy sense fell upon these undecided twenty-two million voters. They simply could not shake the burden to vote. They weren't sure who they would vote for, but they had to do something. Barna's book, *The Day Christians Changed America*, analyzed the election results this way: "Twenty-four hours before the election, undecided Christians were praying. For them, it was a roll of the dice. They had no idea what kind of president Trump would be. He may be crazy; but their only other choice was Hillary, and she was wicked. Crazy or wicked—which way should they go?"[3] They didn't know what Trump would do; he could possibly make things worse. But they *knew* Hillary would lead America further down the path of unrighteousness and destruction. Here's the amazing thing. Many entered the voting booth not sure what to do, but they wanted change. Out of 138 million voters, this one group flipped the vote. That's the power of a remnant. To appreciate the power of a remnant, take a look at these graphics.

2　*https://www.usnews.com/news/the-run-2016/articles/2016-11-14/the-10-closest-states-in-the-2016-election" U.S. News & World Report online, 2016. https://www.usnews.com/news/the-run-2016/articles/2016-11-14/the-10-closest-states-in-the-2016-election*

3　George Barna, *The Day Christians Changed America: How Christian Conservatives Put Trump in the White House and Redirected America's Future.* (United in Purpose Education, 2017).

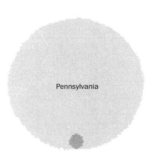

**Trump Won
Pennsylvania
By 68,236 votes**

**A remnant made
the difference**

**Trump won PA by
68,236 votes**

**That's - 0.01% of
all votes**

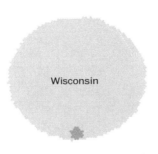

**Trump Won Wisconsin
By 27,257 votes**

**A remnant
made the
difference**

**27,257 votes in
Wisconsin**

**That's - 0.009% of
all votes**

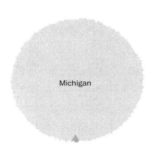

**Trump Won Michigan
By 13,080 votes**

**A remnant made
the difference**

**13,080 votes in
Michigan**

**That's - 0.002% of
all votes**

Stephen Strang wrote about this miraculous Trump win in the August 2020 edition of *Charisma* magazine saying,

> What happened in 2016 was a direct response to the prayers of the righteous here in America and beyond. It was a last-minute reprieve. It was a period where God was willing to show his mercy, His grace and his love and give us just a little more time. The time was given not only to the American people but more so to the American church! Our mandate was simple: **do not act as if it's business as usual. God wanted us to repent as a nation and as a church.** To begin to lead the culture again in accordance with the truth of the Word of God. To once again stand for righteousness and **push back against the demonic agenda we** were under so we could change the trajectory in which this nation was headed. At that time we had seen decades of moral decline, a prolonged anti-God anti-Christianity movement and a death culture that continued to celebrate the murder of our most innocent societal members—our babies!"[4]

What we failed to realize was our mandate. We thought President Trump was the central actor in the story of America, but he isn't. He is a Cyrus, the instrument God provided in a window of grace so the people of God could do what only Christians can do. Trump isn't called to be the spiritual reformer for America; that is our job. We are the ones who have authority at the gates of hell. Our job is to heal, deliver, and restore whatever is collapsing in culture. We must build a spiritual house for the nation and restore its cultural walls and gates. The Chaos Code has revealed to us that the main actor in the story of nations is not Cyrus Trump, but the body of Christ, delivering to Christ His inheritance, the harvest of nations. In his article, Strang posed a series of questions that we need to be asking ourselves in this election cycle: "As we look back at the last four years, has the American Church done its part of the bargain? Have we risen up in prayer, fasting, and standing for righteousness? Have we been outspoken

---

4 Stephen Strang, "The Spiritual Reality of COVID-19." *Charisma Magazine.* Charisma Media, Aug 2020. https://www.charismamag.com/spirit/ spiritual-warfare/45882-stephen-strang-the-spiritual-reality-of-covid-19.

from the pulpit and pushed back against the assignment of the enemy to morally bankrupt our culture and attack our children's minds and identities? Have we made progress in taking our country back from falling off the moral abyss? Have we done enough?"[5]

EXTENSION OF TIME

Satan needs to destroy America. It's his one obstruction. "America is a firewall that prevents the one event Satan craves most: global anarchy."[6] As every devil in hell is manifesting to remove Trump from office, the remnant will once again need to respond and plead with God in the courts of heaven for an extension of grace, mercy, and most importantly, time. Satan is desperate to change the times and seasons. He wants to shut Cyrus Trump's window of mercy over America. God's intention is to save America, but this does not seem to be an issue settled in heaven. There has to be a successful tipping point, just as there was when the angel Gabriel was able to break through in Daniel's time. The Lord is telling us that we are locked in a moment of strenuous wrestling in an undecided match. That's what the chaos assault has been leading us up to all along.

The prophet Daniel gives an insight into the personality and mystery of the antichrist spirit that desires to thwart God's plans: *"And he **shall speak great words against the most High**, and **shall wear out the saints** of the most High, and **think to change times and laws**."*[7] This spirit seeks to disrupt, alter, and modify the time and season of God's activity. Satan wants to make alterations in God's times concerning America; he wants to interrupt the timing of its destiny.

We need to pray that God will give us an extension of time just like He did with King Hezekiah. When King Hezekiah was sick, God told him he was going to die[8] ; but Hezekiah turned his face to the wall, cried out to God, and asked for an extension of time. In His mercy, God changed

---

5 Stephen Strang, "The Spiritual Reality of COVID-19." *Charisma Magazine.* Charisma Media, Aug 2020. https://www.charismamag.com/spirit/ spiritual-warfare/45882-stephen-strang-the-spiritual-reality-of-covid-19.

6 Mario Murillo, "Vessels of Fire and Glory." Destiny Image. 2020

7 Daniel 7:25 (KJV).

8 Adapted from 2 Kings 20:1–11.

his mind and told Hezekiah he would give him fifteen more years on the earth. As a sign of His promise, He moved the sundial back ten degrees. The tears of a king caused God to give Hezekiah the gift of time.

The story of Hezekiah teaches us that God's ferocious mercy can intervene. God wants to extend mercy to America—not judgment. He wanted the remnant in Jerusalem to recover their economy and not go broke! The modern-day remnant has been praying for an awakening, and I believe God is moving in the midst of the shaking. Heaven is revealing the root and the fruit of what we are up against as a nation and God is laying the axe to the root of the tree. Our nation is sick, and without an extension of God's mercy—and time—we face the premature death of America.

THE CURRENCY OF MERCY

The United States is a young nation in comparison to China, Russia, the UK, France, Italy, Germany, Greece, and the nations of Europe. America is too young to die. In 2016 God revealed to Dutch Sheets that He wants to show America mercy, not judgment. He wrote:

When describing the elections, I use the word "mercy" very intentionally. For others and myself, three profound occurrences caused this word to become our primary appeal to heaven during that season.

Firstly, in February while praying at the White House, two friends and I had an angelic visitation. In response to our prayers and decrees, the angel simply said, "Mercy, mercy, mercy, mercy, mercy, mercy." [Yes, six times.]

Secondly, a few weeks later, an intercessor shared a dream she had received from the Lord regarding me. "In the dream," she related, "You kept declaring, I have tapped into a root of mercy."

Then, two weeks before the 2016 presidential election, a trusted pastor and friend had a vision while watching our Appeal to Heaven conference online. As we prayed crying out for mercy, he began to see coins raining down all around me. Eventually, I was ankle deep in silver coins. When he looked at them closely, they all had the word "MERCY" over their various pictures. One coin in particular had George Washington on the front, with the word "MERCY" over him; the other side had the American flag pictured with the words "New Glory" over it. As you know, a nickname for our flag is "Old Glory." There is "new glory" coming to "old glory." Then my friend heard the words, "Mercy is our new currency."[9]

I quote Dutch's 2016 vision because I believe it's true. Mercy is more than undeserved kindness. It is either a full pardon from a crime you are guilty of committing or it is a stay of execution. The angel's declaration of *"mercy"* six times also connects to the six forty-year cycles of mercy that America has experienced since 1776. The 2016 election cycle would have been exactly 240 years since 1776 and that's six cycles of mercy. To understand the forty year cycle, consider that forty is the number of testing and transition: forty years in the wilderness as Israel stepped into its Promised Land, forty days of Goliath taunting until David showed up, and forty days of Jesus's fasting and prayer prior to launching His ministry. So far, we have had six cycles of mercy since our declaration to become a nation. **America's six cycles of mercy are complete, but the seventh cycle of God's mercy still hangs in the balance.** The coins falling from heaven represent two things. First, they represent the currency of time, like years given to Hezekiah. Second, the coins represent the currency of sacrifice. They are the sacrifices of men and women who came before us and gave so much for our nation, the obedience of American missionaries to share the gospel, and the times America has stood for freedom and peace in the world They are also the prayers and gifts sown to God's purposes. This is why I think the face of George Washington was on one of the coins; it represents the life of a man who gave everything to the establishment of a nation with true religious freedom; a sheep nation. These are the coins being poured out as a currency of mercy.

The outcome of the devil's aggressive assault on America is not yet decided because something is required of us as the scales are being weighed in the balance. Dutch ends by saying, "We must, at this strategic and opportune time in history, continue to cry out for mercy. We must also pray for our leaders, especially Mr. Trump; we must ask for wisdom,

---

9 Dutch Sheets, "Mercy is Our New Currency." *Dutch Sheets Ministries.* iTech Solutions, 21 Dec. 2016. https://rallycall.net/mercy-is-our-new-currency/.

revelation, humility, and boldness. Let's steward America's new birth like we would a newborn baby. Let us become a John Knox–type company of reforming intercessors: 'Give us America or we die!'"[10] God is wanting to release a *new glory* over America, and the remnant has a vote to cast in the spiritual and the natural—we can yet prevail.

AN APPEAL TO HEAVEN

There are three unusual moments when scales are shifted toward *mercy* and away from *judgment*.

First, **the nation of Israel carries a very real spiritual currency.** The Word of God in this matter is clear, as the Lord spoke to Abraham, "*I will bless those who bless you, and whoever curses you I will curse*"[11] Rulers and nations will determine their own destiny by how they respond to Israel. America has stood with Israel since 1948 and voted for its recognition as a nation. This support reached a unique climax under Donald Trump's bold stand to support Israel. This is our strongest petition to heaven! President Trump was the first president to move an embassy to Jerusalem and argue for Israel's right to recognition. He supported Israel's right to the protection of the Golan Heights. In January of 2020 he took down Iran's number-one terrorist mastermind against Israel, General Soleimani. Trump even brokered peace deals between Israel and the UAE (United Arab Emirates) and Israel and Bahrain. For these two historic agreements even his critics were forced to recognize him as worthy of consideration for the Nobel Peace Prize.

Trump has also fought for Christians around the world. An American pastor, Pastor Andrew Brunson, had been jailed in Turkey for two years with no hope of rescue. That is, until Trump went to work on his negotiations after meeting with Brunson's wife and daughter. On July 26, 2018, US Vice President Pence called Turkish President Erdoğan and told him to release Pastor Brunson or face significant sanctions. Turkey would not budge, so Donald Trump decided to impose sanctions on two Turkish government officials who were involved in the detention of Brunson. When they still resisted,

---

10 Dutch Sheets, "Mercy is Our New Currency." *Dutch Sheets Ministries.* iTech Solutions, Dec. 21, 2016, https://rallycall.net/mercy-is-our-new-currency/.

11 Genesis 12:3 (NIV).

THE DAY CHRISTIANS CHANGED HISTORY

on August 9, President Trump raised a tariff on Turkish products. Erdoğan followed suit with tariffs on US products, but Turkey couldn't compete and experienced the worst inflation since 2003. Erdoğan released Brunson.

After the pastor's release, Trump went to the United Nations on September 23, 2019, and was shocked to discover that he was the first US president to host a meeting on religious liberty. He told them he was also shocked to discover that 80 percent of the world's population lives in countries where religious freedom is "threatened, restricted, or even banned." Trump declared, "We're standing up for almost 250 million Christians around the world who are persecuted for their faith. It is estimated that 11 Christians are killed every day for the following the teachings of Christ — I mean, just think of this: Eleven Christians a day, for following the teachings of Christ. Who would even think that's possible in this day and age? Who would think it's possible?"[12]

In the entire history of the Oval Office, Trump has proven to be the best friend to Christians and to Jews. America needs a miracle and it may be that God in His mercy will take into account the faithfulness of this administration to His people Israel and Christians. **If there was ever a time we needed to draw on this heavenly account it is now**, reminding the Lord of His promise: "*I will bless those who bless you, and whoever curses you I will curse*"[13]

Second, **we must appeal to God's own name and reputation.** This is perhaps the greatest secret to prevailing with God in prayer because it has *nothing* to do with our simply seeking to avert personal hardship; it has everything to do with God and His name. Moses did just this when the Israelites sinned and God wanted to judge the people. Moses stood in the gap between the people and God's judgment:

> *And the Lord said to Moses, "I have seen this people, and they are indeed stiff-necked people. Now leave Me alone, so that My anger may burn against them and consume them. Then I will make you into a great*

---

12 "Remarks By President Trump At The United Nations Event On Religious Freedom." Whitehousegov, 23 Sept 2019. https://www.whitehouse.gov/briefings-statements/remarks-president-trump-united-nations-event-religious-freedom-new-york-ny/
13 Genesis 12:3 (NIV).

nation." But Moses sought the favor of the Lord his God, saying, "O Lord, why does Your anger burn against Your people, whom You brought out of the land of Egypt with great power and a mighty hand?"[14]

Note, the Lord said, *"Leave me alone."* Moses was standing in the path of God's judgment, thwarting His intention toward the people of Israel. Like Moses, the intercessor stands between God and the people. Note that God calls the Israelites this people, not My people. God always referred to them as My people when he delivered them from Egypt. Moses redirected God's language back to *"Your people."*

Then Moses brings up the ultimate prayer strategy: an appeal to **God's reputation.** The Lord's prayer opens with God's reputation: *"Our Father which art in heaven, **Hallowed be thy name**."*[15] God's name comes before our requests.

Moses petitioned: ***"Why should the Egyptians declare, 'He (God) brought them out with evil intent, to kill them in the mountains and wipe them from the face of the earth'?** Turn from Your fierce anger and relent from doing harm to **Your people**."*[16]

This second factor is the appeal to God's name and reputation. "What will the nations say about America, Lord?" Some might say, God's reputation requires that He judge America, but I ask, what will the nations say when the brightest light for Christianity goes out?

What will it look like when a president who has stood so boldly and so decisively for Christians and for Israel on the world stage fails? What will the heathen, the false religions, and the atheists say when this president's nation is shredded? What will the heathen think, Lord? This man stood for the Church; he fought for your people. What will the unbeliever think about the faith this president honored? This man stood for Israel. What will the enemies of Israel say about the God of Israel if this man is defeated and dishonored? *In judgment, remember mercy.*[17] Has the Lord not said, *"For I will honor those who honor Me, but those who despise Me will be disdained?"*[18]

---

14 Exodus 32:9–11 (Berean Study Bible).
15 Matthew 6:9 (KJV).
16 Exodus 32:12 (Berean Study Bible).
17 Adapted from Habakkuk 3:2.
18 1 Samuel 2:30 (Berean Study Bible).

"If anyone serves Me, the Father will honor him"[19] Please hear the point—our deliverance from adversity should be grounded in **God's own reputation.** We need to pray with this in mind for America.

Third, we must tap into America's covenant roots that were formed in the soil of this land in its beginning. The first settlers of Jamestown went ashore on April 29, 1607, for the express purpose of dedicating the continent to the glory of God. In anticipation of this moment, they crossed the ocean with one special item from England—a rough-hewn seven-foot wooden cross. The colonists and sailors placed the cross in the sand, gathered around it, and held the first formal prayer service in Virginia to give thanks for God's mercy on their endeavor. Guided by Rev. Robert Hunt, they dedicated the land to the glory of God, declaring, "...From these very shores the gospel shall go forth to not only this New World, but the entire world." Don't believe the lies that America was solely a secular experiment; it was built on the foundation of settlers who were made up of entrepreneurs and people of profound Christian faith. It is a divine initiative intended to be part of the Lord's inheritance as a sheep nation.

THE 400-YEAR COVENANT

On September 16, 1620, after two failed attempts, 102 passengers embarked on a grueling ten-week journey from England to the New World. The ship was the Mayflower, and it was heading for Virginia. Its passengers, the colonists, were half religious separatists and half entrepreneurs. The religious half were Puritans fleeing from religious persecution at the hands of King James I of England. This was, in fact, a church relocation project!

The Atlantic crossing was so treacherous that the ninety-foot Mayflower was blown more than 500 miles off course by the rough seas and storms. After sixty-six days at sea, they didn't arrive in Virginia; instead they arrived in Massachusetts. After arriving so far north, some of the non-Puritan passengers (the Puritans referred to them as "Strangers") refused to recognize any rules, since there was no official government over them. To prevent an uprising, the Pilgrims determined that they needed to

---

19 John 12:26 (Berean Study Bible).

establish their own government. New England needed some sort of agreed structure if they were to survive together in the unknown land.

Before anyone disembarked the Mayflower, they created an agreement, a type of social contract, called the Mayflower Compact. It bound the signers to a "civil body politic," a group of citizens acting together as a law-making body. The Mayflower Compact was the very first time the idea of self-government was expressed in the New World. This was a powerful seed planted in the soil. It established constitutional law and the rule of the majority, proving to be a precursor to American democracy. It clearly explains why the New World was settled and the spiritual intention behind the expedition. They wrote in the Mayflower Compact:

> **"IN THE NAME OF GOD...** *We, whose names are underwritten...* **Having undertaken for the Glory of God, and Advancement of the Christian Faith**... *Do by these Presents, solemnly and mutually,* **in the Presence of God and one another, covenant and combine ourselves together into a civil Body** *Politick, for our better Ordering and Preservation, and* **Furtherance of the Ends aforesaid**"[20] *(emphasis added).*

On November 21, 1620, the compact was signed. **We are now about to enter the 400th anniversary of this covenant this November!** This country was cultivated by men and women undertaking the journey for the Glory of God and advancement of the Christian Faith! As we cry out to God for the nation, we should remind the Lord, one another, and the devil himself that we are aligned with the synergy of those who have gone before us. Only one hundred years ago, when the covenant was renewed on the 300th anniversary of the Mayflower landing, Governor Calvin Coolidge, who later became president, said:

> The compact which they signed was an event of the greatest importance. It was the foundation of liberty based on law and order, and that tradition has been steadily upheld. They drew up a form of government which has been designated as **the first**

---

20 William Braford, *The Mayflower Compact.* Nov. 11, 1620, https://nationalcenter. org/MayflowerCompact.html.

real constitution of modern times. It was democratic, an acknowledgment of liberty under law and order and the giving to each person the right to participate in the government, while they promised to be obedient to the laws.[21]

But the really wonderful thing was that they had the power and strength of character to abide by it and live by it from that day to this. Some governments are better than others. **But any form of government is better than anarchy, and any attempt to tear down government is an attempt to wreck civilization.**[22]

The quote by Calvin Coolidge is profound in light of where we are as a nation. Liberty and our fundamental freedoms thrive under law and order, not anarchy and chaos. It needs the soil of law and order to grow and flourish. The other fascinating point Coolidge makes is that law and order mean nothing if people do not have the power and strength of character to abide by them. This is the fabric of America the left is looking to tear apart. They would have you believe that unchecked human desire is freedom. It isn't. It is a formula for anarchy and societal collapse.

On the Mayflower there were two different sources of moral authority contending for influence. The two factions on board give us an insight into the spiritual battle in our nation today. One stream runs deep into our roots in the Reformation and Puritan intellectual and devotional life. The other stream draws from the European Enlightenment—those who rejected the Bible as the source of transcendent authority. The children of the Enlightenment thought of themselves as more reasonable. These were the ancestors of today's progressives.

This Mayflower Compact of 1620 was a clear statement about the dedication of America to the Lord. It is just one of the *many* stories in the archives of history that reveals the covenant roots of this land. As we draw

---

21 Quoted in Mark Lutter, "Charter Cities and America." *Charter Cities Institute,* July 7, 2020. https://www.chartercitiesinstitute.org/post/charter-cities-and-america.

22 "Learn From Pilgrims Coolidge Admonishes." *New York Herald,* 23 Nov 1920. https://tile.loc.gov/storage-services/service/ndnp/dlc/batch_dlc_quercitron_ver01/data/sn83045774/00271744109/1920112301/0704.pdf

near to the 400th anniversary of the Mayflower Compact in November, we need to petition God for the future of our nation based on these rich covenantal foundations laid by the sacrifice of men and women before us. America's spiritual inheritance, its covenants with God, and the generations of Christians that came before us are an even stronger appeal that divine providence would once again intervene and grant us the gift of time, for the sake of the Church and the nations of the earth.

These are the three prayer strategies we need to bring to the courts of Heaven to petition God for an extension of mercy. We have assembled a prayer guide based on these and other key strategies that you can download at GodsChaosCode.com/prayer.

A VOTE IS A SPIRITUAL ACT

Last, we **must** activate our faith and plant it like a seed. James exhorts us that, "*faith without works is dead.*"[23] This means that faith without corresponding action is impotent. If we are going to fight for the destiny of America, then we are going to need to take some sort of spiritual action, and that action is manifest when we vote for candidates that honor the policies that honor God. The reality is political issues are spiritual issues. Political issues are faith issues. *Never* vote based on a party or a personality. It is remarkable how many Christians fail to discern political and cultural issues from a Biblical perspective. Your vote is your "amen" and agreement in the earth. Never give your support to anyone based on looks, ethnicity, personality, or party. God says, "*Do not judge by appearances.*"[24] It is remarkable to hear Christians fumbling around because they don't like Trump's tone or tweets. Go beneath personality, gender, skin color or looks. Go deeper than following the herd and voting for the same political party as your family and friends. Don't be controlled by news cycles. Guard against the increasing power of manipulation in social media, print and broadcasts. Remember, on the day Jesus stood before Pontius Pilate, the devil had a louder group screaming. Always look first at the policies and the platform underneath the politician. Discover the platform! Here is a voter guide that compares both platforms.

---

23 James 2:—26 (NKJV).
24 John 7:24 (NKJV).

2020 PRESIDENTIAL ELECTION VOTER GUIDE

AS ONE America
ASONEAMERICA.COM

	DONALD TRUMP	R	JOE BIDEN	D
LATE TERM ABORTION Unrestricted, late-term abortions	OPPOSES[1]		SUPPORTS[14]	
RELIGIOUS FREEDOM Federal protection of individuals' and/or entities' religious convictions	SUPPORTS[2]		OPPOSES[15]	
GUN CONTROL Increased gun control regulations	OPPOSES[3]		SUPPORTS[16]	
SUPREME COURT JUSTICES Appointments of justices who interpret the Constitution by adhering to the framers' original intent and text	SUPPORTS[4]		OPPOSES[17]	
PRISON REFORM Reduced mandatory minimums, commuted sentences and rehabilitation	SUPPORTS[5]		SUPPORTS[18]	
PARENTAL CHOICE IN EDUCATION Funding for charter schools and/or vouchers	SUPPORTS[6]		OPPOSES[19]	
IMMIGRATION Controlling U.S. borders and defunding sanctuary cities	SUPPORTS[7]		OPPOSES[20]	
LAW AND ORDER Deployment of law-enforcement and federal assistance to riot-impacted communities	SUPPORTS[8]		OPPOSES[21]	
TAX CUTS To stimulate economic recovery	SUPPORTS[9]		OPPOSES[22]	
ISRAEL U.S. Embassy in Jerusalem	SUPPORTS[10]		SUPPORTS[23]	
NEW GREEN DEAL Comprehensive climate change regulations	OPPOSES[11]		SUPPORTS[24]	
WOMEN'S SPORTS Allowing biological male athletes who identify as female to participate in girls' sports	OPPOSES[12]		SUPPORTS[25]	
PLANNED PARENTHOOD Federal funding of Planned Parenthood and other abortion providers	OPPOSES[13]		SUPPORTS[26]	

SEE MILLIONVOICES.ORG FOR FOOTNOTES

THIS VOTER GUIDE IS 501(C)(3) COMPLIANT AND APPROVED FOR DISTRIBUTION BY 501(C)(3) ORGANIZATIONS, INCLUDING CHURCHES. THE PURPOSE OF THIS GUIDE IS TO EDUCATE VOTERS, NOT TO ENDORSE ANY PARTICULAR CANDIDATE.

→ You can get your copy at: GodsChaosCode.com/vote ←

When evaluating how to vote you need to turn the rock over and see what's crawling around underneath. Start with biblical principles and sanctified common sense, knowing God's Word speaks to every political and policy issue we face. There are four simple things to look at.

Principles → Platform → Policies → Politician (In that order)

Many Christians choose not to vote because they don't think it will make a difference, especially if they live in states dominated by progressive ideology. What they fail to realize is that their vote means something, it is a seed they get to plant in the soil of America. It is a statement of faith. Would you decide not to pray for the lost at your job because so many unbelievers dominate your workplace? That would be madness.

No matter who the candidate or what the legislation, your vote is a spiritual veto or authorization. Indecision is a decision not to decide! It's a decision to let an unbeliever shape culture. A physical vote is a tangible declaration that says, "Regardless of the outcome, I am planting a seed for God's will to be done in America!" As G.K. Chesterton said, "I do not believe in a fate that falls on men however they act; but I do believe in a fate that falls on them unless they act."[25] It is time the silent majority made its voice known.

---

25 "Quotation Celebration." WordPress, 5 Jan 2018. https://quotationcelebration. wordpress.com/2018/01/05/i-do-not-believe-in-a-fate-that-falls-on-men-however-they-act-but-i-do-believe-in-a-fate-that-falls-on-them-unless-they-act-g-k-chesterton/

CHAPTER 10

AS ONE!

"Lock your shields!"[1]
—*Maximus, Gladiator*

A shift is happening in the atmosphere over America. You can sense it and see it. Heaven and hell are regrouping and colliding in the heavenlies as the body of Christ likewise regroups in the whirlwinds preceding the gathering storm.

What are the angelic hosts doing? You can see it revealed in the activity of the Church on earth. There is a new mind-set beginning to emerge. Western civilization looks to be crashing around us. More than once I have heard people say, "Why doesn't someone do something?" It is almost as if a leadership void exists in the Church, felt so palpably that there is widespread agreement among us that there is no strong voice standing in the gap. Two candidates collide as the physical expression of this ideological contest enters its most ominous final days.

In the midst of this cacophony of voices and world events, a movement is emerging as a triumphant remnant step out of their fragmented battalions, take their stand, and lock their shields in unity—*as one*! In the midst of this are leaders of ministry networks, megachurches, and local churches shaking up the status quo in their communities.

---

1 *Gladiator*. Directed by Ridley Scott, performances by Russell Crowe, Joaquin Phoenix, Connie Nielsen, Oliver Reed, and Dijmon Hounsou. Dreamworks and Universal Pictures. 2000.

WHAT WE ARE UP AGAINST

Paul warned Timothy in the second letter to his young protégé that the church was heading into difficult waters. Perhaps with an eye on coming imperial persecution, he wrote: *"Indeed, all who desire to live godly in Christ Jesus will be persecuted. But evil men and **impostors** will proceed from bad to worse, **deceiving and being deceived**."*[2] The word *impostor* is interesting: the root word describes the spell of a sorcerer or a seductive impostor who juggles words. Paul did not hold out the idea that these men would change. Rather, he predicted that they would get worse. He saw this as an inevitability, based on his understanding of the last days.

"But know this, in the last days perilous times will come because men are lovers of their own selves."[3] In such a case, revival in the church must be welded to reformation so that a limit can be put on the influence of those persuasive imposters who will *"wax worse and worse."*[4] Curiously, Paul put the conflict into the context of a political confrontation: *"Just as Jannes and Jambres opposed Moses, so also these men oppose the truth. They are depraved in mind and disqualified from the faith. But they will not advance much further. For just like Jannes and Jambres, their folly will be plain to everyone."*[5]

Who were Jannes and Jambres? They were the dark-arts magicians of Pharaoh, who resisted Moses and Aaron when God sent them with the message, *"Let My people go!"* Jannes and Jambres were the political opposition in Pharaoh's court. When Aaron performed a sign or wonder, *"Pharaoh called the wise men and sorcerers and magicians of Egypt, and they also did the same things by their magic arts."*[6] Paul is saying that just as Jannes and Jambres drew on occult powers to resist God's will, we can step into these contests having the same hope in our current confrontation that *"their folly will be plain to everyone."* [7]

When we say there is ***spiritual warfare over the nation***, we should be clear about how practical the outworking of this is in terms of the way

---

2 2 Timothy 3:12–13 (NASB).

3 Adapted from 2 Timothy 3:1–2 (KJV).

4 2 Timothy 3:13 (KJV).

5 2 Timothy 3:8–9 (Berean Study Bible).

6 Exodus 7:11 (Berean Study Bible).

7 2 Timothy 3:9 (Berean Study Bible).

these forces are embodied in people and organizations. A vast resistance was launched in 2016, just five days after the election. The minds of those in that resistance were and are under the influence of a strange delusion. What started out once as political football has descended into another territory. Trump opposition starts by *deceiving* others in a news cycle but descends into *being deceived* by a paranoid spirit. It is a deception that is revealed in all their communication that you will see in their publications and transcripts. They are the architects behind the Democrat media complex, delivering their message based on the left-leaning Media Matters for America talking points. This doesn't mean Republicans are virtuous, but it is an open "secret" that Democrats play offense and Republicans defense.

This 2016 resistance was organized by *Democracy Alliance* to analyze the loss, win the midterms, and take out and remove conservative social media and news organizations, while relentlessly assaulting Trump's credibility and progress. Their purpose was to do all this while moving the Democratic Party further to the political left. They strategized how they could undermine, accuse, discredit, and attack President Donald Trump and the "basket of deplorables"[8] who elected him. Little did I know when I introduced the term *Trump Derangement* in 2015 that the madness would be so profound. The leftists discovered that the best way to influence the Democratic Party was to take it over. This resistance army was composed of 172 well-funded and centrally controlled organizations.

David Horowitz explains their secretive Mandarin Oriental Hotel meeting:

> *The entire event was organized and paid for by George Soros's "Democracy Alliance." The Alliance is a coalition of 110 billionaires who have each pledged to contribute $200,000 a year toward left-wing causes. For decades, Soros has worked to shape the politics of the Democratic Party by creating a coalition of left-wing groups that will support his agendas. The coalition consists of trade unions, political movements like the Marxoid "Working Families Party," philanthropic and advocacy groups like the*

---

8   Katie Rielly, "Hillary Clinton Basket Of Deplorables." *Time* online, 10 September 2016. https://time.com/4486502/hillary-clinton-basket-of-deplorables-transcript/.

Tides Foundation, blacklist organizations and smear sites like Blood Money and the Southern Poverty Law Center, and violent street communists who fomented anti-capitalist protests and anti-police riots, like "Occupy Wall Street" and "Black Lives Matter." Their Mandarin Oriental gathering lasted four days. Among its attendees were several hundred activists and politicians like House Democratic leader Nancy Pelosi, Senator Elizabeth Warren, and Congressional Progressive Caucus co-chairman Keith Ellison.[9]

According to a *Daily Mail* reporter who was present at the meeting, some sessions focused intensely on winning control of Congress in the midterm elections.[10] Other work groups focused on a multi-pronged strategy to thwart each appointment made by President-elect Trump in his 100-day plan, which they referred to as "a terrifying assault on President Obama's achievements—and our progressive vision for an equitable and just nation." Commented the reporter: "If the agenda is any indication, liberals plan full-on trench warfare against Trump from Day One."[11]

The outworkings of this meeting started just a few days after it happened. President Trump's inauguration was boycotted by seventy Congressmen, making Donald Trump the first president to be dishonored in this manner. All of this was done against a backdrop of DC violence and looting by Antifa, a story that was neglected by the Democrat media complex. Trump would also be denied the customary 100 days given to get on his feet in his new role.

The first Soros-funded anti-Trump action was the "Woman's March" that took place the day after the inauguration. One wonders if the Jewish women participating knew it was led by an anti-Israel activist and terrorist supporter. The "Not My President" protest accused Trump of being racist,

---

9   David Horowitz, *Blitz* (West Palm Beach: Humanix, 2017).

10 Francesca Chambers, "Soros Group Bands with Mega Donors to Resist Trump and Take Back Power for Democrats." *Daily Mail,* Nov. 16, 2016. https://www.dailymail.co.uk/news/article-3942556/Soros-bands-donors-resist-Trump-power.html

11 Jason Easly "Payback Time: Democrats and Liberals Plan Tota Trench Warfare On Trump." PoliticusUSA, 14 November 2016. https://www.politicususa.com/2016/11/14/payback-time-democrats-liberals-plan-total-trench-warfare-trump.html.

sexist, and anti-immigrant. With several million activists in 600 cities, it was the largest demonstration in US history. The Democracy Alliance has been the hidden hand at work since day one.

What should strike all of us is the realization that the Christian community simply—watched. Many just became sideline Twitter post critics. That this occurred when Trump had 85 percent of the evangelical support and after millions of believers saw Donald Trump as a reprieve from national judgment is a cause for reflection.

Things went from bad to worse with the disastrous 2018 midterms that resulted in two years of one-sided investigations by Mueller and impeachment drama over a phone call to the Ukraine. Had the Church not *slept* through the critical midterms, history would have been different. I have spent the last few years analyzing the Church and the nature of our divisions. I discovered that there are three reasons why Christians self-sabotage when it comes to winning strategic national battles. As the saying goes, "Leftists don't like each other but work together; Christians love each other but won't work together."

LOVER, WARRIOR, STATESMAN

Scholars see the church locked in three cultural paradigms: Defensive Against, Relevant To, and Purity From. **These paradigms represent how the Church engages culture. They correspond to three aspects of Jesus' personality. I like to simplify them into** *the Lover, the Warrior, and the Statesman.* They embody three indispensable attributes: the warrior's *courage*, the lover's *purity*, and statesman's *wisdom*. Combined together, the body of Christ puts Jesus on display. **When the three come together,** *as one*, **the world will see Jesus.**

- **Warrior (Defensive Against)**: This company of believers is in full-out battle mode right now. Twenty-seven years ago, James Kennedy said: "If Christians are not involved as salt and light in our culture, we will one day wake up to find our freedom to live as Christians gone. The Barbarians will be at the church door, and we won't be able to have our separatist pietist meetings. Our society will become increasingly corrupt, godless, and hostile, until people finally break down the doors of the church and haul the Christians away. That's what happened in Russia ... they had

70 years to rue that failure."[12] Kennedy warned that if we ignore the cultural mandate, then we may have a government increasingly hostile to Christianity.

James Kennedy's "Defensive-Against" plan challenged pastors to encourage their congregations to be involved with both evangelism and legislation. Some ask "What right do Christians have to impose our morality on others?" All legislation is the imposition of someone's morality upon others. Kennedy went on to say that progressives "are busily engaged in imposing their version of morality on this country."[13] The "Defensive-Against" leaders see two tracks: as light, we illuminate the world with the truth of the gospel; and as salt, we prevent or slow down the utter corruption of an already-corrupted society.

- **Statesman (Relevance To)**: This paradigm seeks to speak into contemporary culture by coming alongside and ministering to "felt needs" with relevant sermons and services. The church services are structured for the potential seeker. In truth, more evangelism happens in these corporate gatherings than occurs on the streets. For this reason, cultural controversies are avoided. While Rick Warren's church wrote the pastor's blueprint for this approach, it was Jack Hayford who carried the argument. Hayford wrote in 1993 right after Bill Clinton was elected president: "The November 1993 election formalized a lower moral baseline than we've ever admitted to as a nation. But we don't gain anything by making enemies of society, by berating others for ignoring our moral standards. Little evangelistic fruit will result from our reminding society that America once had superior morals and was founded on the Judeo-Christian ethic. We take a stance of proclamation more than protest."[14] Jack did not argue for a watered-down gospel but

12 Quoted by Jimmy Long. *Emerging Hope: A Strategy for Reaching Postmodern Generations.* InterVarsity Press, 1993, p. 31.

13 Ibid.

14 Leonard Sweet, "What the World Needs Now." *Christianity Today,* 2020. https://www.christianitytoday.com/pastors/1993/winter/93l2020.html.

did challenge the public nature of Christian political engagement. Regarding the calling of people to repentance, he said, "Where should we do that? John the Baptist called those who came to him to repentance. Calling people to turn to God when they come inside the venue of your ministry is one thing, but it's another to parade in protest because worldlings don't meet the divine standards we're holding in their face. In their environment they don't care, and they didn't ask us to come."[15] Hayford is saying that the proper place to call people to repentance is inside the sanctuary. This, however, would be problematic for the church-growth model—the difficulty being that churches found that it was better to focus on felt-needs messages that addressed the day-to-day struggles of people than to speak about doctrines that focus elsewhere on sanctification, sin, and so forth. As the sanctuary became ground zero for seeker evangelism, the first century model of *"reprove, rebuke, exhort with all longsuffering and patience"*[16] seemed incongruent with an evangelism agenda.

Hayford in his "Relevant-To" position contrasts with James Kennedy in terms of teaching people about cultural issues, raising awareness about legislation, and influencing public thinking about policy. To Hayford, "salt" would not manifest as Kennedy suggests in "Defensive Against" as a resistance to the decay of public conscience. Hayford's approach would be "They'll start listening to the truth of God because they've seen the love of God in the way I came to them." [17]

- **Lover (Purity From)**: This paradigm shares the concern of the "Defensive Against" paradigm in its desire to preserve the faith, but this group believes the central task of the church is to extricate and isolate itself as much as possible from the contaminating defilement of this world system. There is a desire to be a witness,

---

15 Ibid.

16 2 Timothy 4:2 (KJV).

17 Leonard Sweet, "What the World Needs Now." *Christianity Today,* 2020. https://www.christianitytoday.com/pastors/1993/winter/9312020.html.

but it is unlikely to occur in intensely secular settings. These are the descendants of Puritan influence who see the world as a great secular and sacred divide. "Purity From" periodically emerges in different forms, such as fundamentalism in one generation or charismatic monasticism in another, engaging the quest for greater detachment from earth while seeking intimacy with God. Some merge "Purity From" with the "Relevance To," hoping to pray for people in order to demonstrate supernatural ministry. Adherents to this view see revival and conversion as the means of changing culture. The flaw here is that while salvation is the most important personal experience, this model alone, even with a harvest, does not translate to cultural change any more than increasing the number of seats on a bus alters the direction of the bus. To do that you need to rotate or convert the drivers. In many nations, Christians are already a majority who are being led by a minority in the drivers' seats.

Looking to Jesus as a model of all three frameworks we see:

- **Jesus as Lover** says, *"I did not come into the world to condemn the world but that the world might be saved."*[18] *"Father forgive them, they don't know what they are doing."*[19] Jesus had a close nurturing relationship with His disciples. At the last supper, John reclined on the breast of Jesus. To identify the one who would betray Him, Jesus put food into Judas's mouth. When the disciple who betrayed Him sought to give a sign about which one they should arrest, the Rabbi was identified with a kiss. Jesus took children up in His arms to bless them. All of this speaks to Jesus the lover.

- **Jesus as Warrior** says, *"For this reason the Son of God was made manifest, that He might destroy the works of the devil."*[20] *"Woe to you, scribes and Pharisees, hypocrites! For you are like whitewashed tombs, which outwardly appear beautiful, but within are full of dead people's bones*

---

18 Adapted from John 3:17 (NKJV).
19 Luke 23:34 (New Heart English Bible).
20 Adapted from 1 John 3:8.

and all uncleanness."[21] *"And He made a scourge of cords, and drove them all out of the temple, with the sheep and the oxen; and He poured out the coins of the money changers and overturned their tables."*[22] The Jewish people expected their Messiah to come as a great military figure but He came as the Lamb of God. At the end of the age God's people expect the Lamb of God to return but Paul says Jesus will be revealed *"with His mighty angels in blazing fire, inflicting vengeance on those who do not know God and do not obey the gospel of our Lord Jesus."*[23] This aspect of the Lord will be revealed as *wrath* prior to His return. *"He will crush kings in the day of His wrath. He will judge the nations."*[24] Jesus the lover and Jesus the warrior are both the same Jesus. Jesus the lover went to war with the devil for the souls of men, and Jesus the warrior laid down His life for that victory.

- **Jesus as Statesman** says, *"Give unto Caesar what is Caesar's and unto God what is God's."*[25] *"Which of you having 1000 soldiers would go against someone with 10,000? You would be better off looking for terms of peace."*[26] Likewise, if someone is taking you to court, see if you can somehow establish common ground and resolve your issue on your way to court.[27] This is the statesman ruler speaking. Jesus the statesman organized the feeding of 5000 by having men sit in companies of 50.

All three paradigms are correct in their own context. "Defensive Against" is the call to *courage* and is the spiritual equivalent of law enforcement, dealing with something criminal. "Relevant To" is the call to *wisdom* and answers the call to be winsome and wise in evangelism and engagement with unbelievers. "Purity From" is the call to *devotion* and speaks to the need that all Christians have to withdraw from the crowd into the

---

21 Matthew 23:27 (ESV).

22 John 2:15

23 2 Thessalonians 1:7–8 (Berean Study Bible).

24 Psalm 110: 5–6 (Berean Study Bible).

25 Adapted from Mark 12:17 (Berean Study Bible).

26 Adapted from Luke 14:31–32.

27 Adapted from Matthew 5:25.

wilderness to sustain intimacy with the Lord. The courageous warrior, devoted lover, and wise ruler seems like the most holistic representation of Christ the church could present.

You will most likely identify with one of these three paradigms. If you're not sure, just look at who is around you. Like attracts like. Yet any one of these three positions, if not flexible, will fail to be *"ready in season and out of season."*[28] Nothing captures the importance of knowing the times and seasons like this quote from one of my mentors, John Kelly: "My biggest regrets are the times I acted like a General when I should have been a Father, and the times I acted like a Father when I should have been a General."[29] All three paradigms must adapt to seasons. Ecclesiastes 3:8 says there is *"a time to love, and a time to hate; a time for war, and a time for peace."*[30] We need to know the season we are living in and unify behind a clarion call in the arena.

MOVING "AS ONE!"

The full picture of our current dilemma in the West was unveiled before my eyes, not in a prophetic vision but in a movie theater. It came alive as I watched the movie *Gladiator*. The story and the moment are worth repeating. Maximus Meridius arrived in Rome earlier in the day among the school of gladiators quietly unloading from their long trip out of North Africa. All heads but one swivel about to gaze upon the marvel of Rome at the height of its power. He proceeded quietly, unimpressed, as he had seen Rome before. His desire to stay hidden was futile, as the fame of this one they call "the Spaniard" preceded him, fed by eyewitnesses of his performance in the arenas of the Roman province of Zucchabar. Rumors of his exploits in Africa had already made him legendary, and Rome was not easily impressed.

Unlike others, this man had a talent for war. He survived three years of contests in arenas and pits, working his way up quickly. He fought with a rare combination of strength and cunning, and a signature dash of pageantry. In earlier days, he had dispatched his adversaries with a savagery that bespoke of some deep-seated personal rage. Over time the

---

28 2 Timothy 4:2 (NKJV).
29 John Kelly. Personal Interview, 2020.
30 Ecclesiastes 3:8 (NIV).

rage subsided, and he became a dispassionate executioner, always finishing off his last combatant with a theatrical flair for the approval of the crowd. Even then, he was different. He did not seek to please the crowd. In fact, he often held the crowd in contempt. A discerning eye might have put it together; the tactics, lethal efficiency, and pageantry were the hallmarks of Roman generals.

Indeed, at an earlier time in his career, Maximus was the commander of the Felix Legions of Rome. As a general, he was the celebrated and trusted servant to the emperor Marcus Aurelius, Rome's kindly and philosophic ruler. His fidelity, while an asset to Aurelius—ever mindful of political intrigues among his generals—was a liability when dealing with the emperor's treacherous son, Commodus. This famous son had murdered his emperor father to seize the throne and then arranged for the execution of Maximus, along with the murder of his wife and son.

En route to his execution, Maximus escaped. He was assumed to be a deserter when he was taken prisoner by a passing slave caravan. Maximus was sold to a school of North African gladiators, where he went underground as a local gladiator in an academy run by a former gladiator-turned-businessman named Proximo. Keeping his identity hidden, Maximus rose through the ranks of gladiatorial contest.

As a distraction to hard economic times, the emperor Commodus had been conducting a month of unusual games. On that particular day, the best of Rome's gladiators met the best of the North Africa gladiators. The impatient mob had swollen to 50,000 in anticipation of the grand crescendo to the month of contests and gore. Scattered applause was heard as Maximus and thirteen others entered the Colosseum, taking their place in the dirt center of the great theater.[31]

Adjusting his eyes to the sun, he briefly scanned the arena and then fixed his cold gaze upon the emperor's box, where the event officially began. The announcer Cassius raises his voice and begins: "On this day, we reach back to hallowed antiquity, to bring you a recreation of the second fall of mighty Carthage! ... On the barren plain of Zama, there stood the

---

31 *Gladiator*. Directed by Ridley Scott, performances by Russell Crowe, Joaquin Phoenix, Connie Nielsen, Oliver Reed, and Dijmon Hounsou, Dreamworks and Universal Pictures, 2000.

invincible armies of the barbarian Hannibal. Ferocious mercenaries and warriors from all brute nations, bent on merciless destruction. Commodus, your emperor, is pleased to give you the barbarian horde!"[32]

The crowd jeered and booed as the remnant in the center of the arena was officially introduced. The men looked about, puzzling over whom they were to fight in an empty arena. But Maximus, who knew the history of battles, had already sized up the situation, recalling how Scipio had defeated Hannibal by the use of cavalry. He shifted his focus upon the gates, calculating how many chariots he and his men would face.

As the announcer continued his introduction, Maximus took charge. He cried out, "Has anyone here ever served in the army?"[33]

A chorus of voices reply yes.

"Good. You can help me. Whatever comes through those gates, we've got a better chance of survival if we work together. Do you understand me? If we stay together, we survive."[34]

At that point Cassius extended his arm once more toward the gates and bellowed, "I'm pleased to bring to you the Legionnaires of Scipio Africanas!"[35]

Upon cue, the gates flew open in a cloud of dust as a furious storm of chariots and archers descended on the small cohort in the middle of the arena. Maximus's steady voice rose above the roar, "Come together … closer … closer … stay as one."[36] The men stunned by the sight began to back up, step-by-step forming a circle. Once in proximity, Maximus shouted, "Lock your shields"[37]—his voice arching over the chaos of the arena. The sound of metallic shields rang out as they locked together. The general now commanded his remnant as he once commanded the Felix Legions.

The archers had already picked off one of Maximus's men while another, not in alignment with the group, was pierced with an arrow through his calf. Maximus broke out of position and pulled him backward

---

32 Ibid.
33 Ibid.
34 Ibid.
35 Ibid.
36 Ibid.
37 Ibid.

into the formation. Like a metallic python, the chariots tightened around the circle as Maximus shouted, "Hold, hold, hold"[38] ... until one chariot broke out and led its horses straight into the circle of men intent on shattering the formation.

At that moment Maximus shouted, "**As one**!" and the men echoed back "**As one**!" ... and with that the chariot hit a wall of metal and was repulsed. The crowd roared in delight! "Well done," the commander snapped approvingly.[39]

The spectators leapt to their feet, rushing in mass to the balcony to get a closer look at the performance of the defiant North African school. The lead chariot wheeled sharply and drove in again with greater force, intent on breaking the circle. Maximus again steadied the soldiers but issued a different command, "Hold, hold, diamond, diamond!"[40] Two men stepped forward, leaning shoulders against tilted shields as they formed a ramp; and with that, the Legionnaire's chariot rolled up over them and overturned, crushing the rider in splinters beneath the chariot and disengaging the horses.

The crowd roared uncontrollably. Gladiators typically fought one on one. Seldom had they seen the spectacle of men moving in such coordinated fashion.

Maximus pointed with his sword, "This column to the chariot. This column stay."[41] The general swiftly mounted one of the harnessed horses, sliced off its harness from the broken chariot, and spurred it forward upon the chariots unexpectedly from behind—striking the riders through their necks one by one until a number had been disabled or killed by him and his column. Beginning first with a few and then picked up by more, the crowd chanted "Maximus! Maximus!"[42] until the words formed a crescendo that filled the arena.

The general continued shouting orders to the troops. "Single column," he pointed to the right. "Single column,"[43] he pointed to the left. No

---

38 Ibid.
39 Ibid.
40 Ibid.
41 Ibid.
42 Ibid.
43 Ibid.

longer in a circle, the men walled in the remaining Legionnaires; closing their ranks, and trapping their opponents they dispatched them quickly. Having won the battle, Maximus upon his white horse raised his sword to acknowledge the crowd, remembering the words he had been told: "Win the crowd and you win your freedom."[44] The patrons of the games were unanimous in their appraisal that this was the most memorable battle ever witnessed in the arena. For the moment it seemed as if all of Rome was stirred. Before the movie closes, Maximus gave his life to free Rome.

OUR CURRENT DAY ARENA

After watching Ridley Scott's *Gladiator* years ago, I left the theater stunned. I said to myself, This isn't a movie; it's a prophetic parable crafted in a filmmaker's studio! The Arts Mountain is always more prophetic than people think. This was a forecast of the crucible facing Christians in our lifetime.

It is not something Christians have not read before. This story echoes the last days of Jesus who entered the arena in Jerusalem to do combat with Hell, and give His life in exchange for the life of His people. Now we are summoned into the arena.

We are being tested in this hour and put on display. Paul said he himself was placed *"on display at the end of the procession, like those condemned to die in the arena. We have been made a **spectacle** to the whole universe, to angels as well as to human beings"*[45] The word "spectacle" is also the word for "theater" but who is the audience? The answer is both angels and human beings.

Peter described, *"Even angels long to look into these things."*[46] The verb "look into" means "to stoop sideways;"[47] It is used for persons standing outside a place who crook their neck or stoop with interest in order to look in on something. This language indicates that the angels stand outside, observing with intense fascination the work of redemption, inasmuch as it is not for them but for man.

---

44 Ibid.

45 1 Corinthians 4:9 (NIV).

46 1 Peter 1:12 (NIV).

47 "parakypsai" (s v). *BibleHub,* The Lockman Foundation, 1998, https://biblehub.com/1_peter/1-12.htm.

The same verb occurs in Luke 24:12 and describes Peter himself, when he stooped to look into the empty sepulcher on the morning of the Lord's resurrection.[48] "To look into" in Greek is literally, "to bend over so as to look deeply into and see to the bottom of a thing."[49] The spirit realm bends over the balcony of heaven so to speak, and watches what unfolds with intense interest during the age of shaking.

As angels are not omniscient, they discover things by observing the Holy Spirit working in and through the Church. Likewise, the spiritual wickedness that rules over territories does not know everything. It watches what the Spirit is doing—in the theater of the Church. As the dispensations of God's work of redemption unfold in history, the Church of Christ is a central actor on the grand stage where heaven's wisdom is put on display "to principalities and to powers in the heavenly places" in the ekklesia, the multifaceted house of God, the Church.

The entire spirit realm is watching the unfolding plan of Christ for this hour. He is laying out plans and dispatching heaven's battalions for the building of a glorious church and the accomplishment of the Great Commission among nations. As we speak, nations are solidifying in their character as goat or sheep nations. The important thing to remember is that *the Church* is the theater that displays God's glorious final acts.

In 1760, Mathew Henry wrote of the "manifold wisdom of God." His commentary speaks to our situation today:

*The divergent tendencies of men, especially in religious matters, were being developed; but … the **manifold wisdom of God** was shown in transforming many of these most diverse elements, unifying them, building them up into a great spiritual body, into a holy, most beautiful, most symmetrical temple. When all things seem to be flying asunder into the most diverse and antagonistic elements, God gives a new turn, as it were, to providence, and lo! a glorious symmetrical and harmonious structure begins to rise.*[50]

---

48 Adapted from Luke 24:12.
49 "parakypsai" (s v). *BibleHub,* The Lockman Foundation, 1998, https://biblehub.com/1_peter/1-12.htm.
50 Matthew Henry, "Pulpit Commentary." BibleHub, 2020. https://biblehub.com/commentaries/pulpit/ephesians/3.htm

In the midst of chaos, God is doing something new. The Lovers and Warriors and Statesmen lock their shields. The covert and the overt form their ranks. The Ezras and Nehemiahs join their assignments. Jesus is building His church for the nations!

A considerable amount of my teaching over the last decade has been focused on the *Seven Mountains*, gates of influence, remnants, networks, and power that is multiplied when we lock our shields. This is the core strategy behind the Chaos Code and the *Seven Mountains* strategy.

As we all take our place it reminds me of Maximus inspirational command "As one!" I am haunted by the words "Whatever comes through those gates, we have a better chance of survival if we work together."[51]

Little did I know at that time that the scene I watched is also the playbook for our battle. Notice the sequence of events and the lessons for us today in six simple movie quotes:

1. **"Whatever comes through those gates, we have a better chance of survival if we work together. If we stay together, we survive."**[52] We must recognize that Christians are becoming an isolated remnant surrounded by an increasingly militant, hostile paganism. The enemy emerges suddenly through wide-open gates. That is the issue. We must win the battle at the gates.

2. **"Come together ... Closer."**[53] Our ability to work together is dependent on our ability to unify. This requires that we learn a new behavior, alien to the Church globally, namely collaboration and unity. This can only come out of mutual respect and trust. You will notice a peculiar new season of divine appointments as you meet key relationships that God is aligning around you for the battle.

3. **"Lock your shields!"**[54] While imprisoned in Rome, the apostle Paul had time to study a soldier's armor. He likened each item to its spiritual counterpart. The shield was made of layers of leather cut to

---

51 Ibid.
52 Ibid.
53 Ibid.
54 Ibid.

the height of the soldier. To each of us is given a measure of faith and a sphere of influence according to our individual assignments. Paul designated this as the "shield of faith."[55] We each have our place. When we bring our individual sphere of influence into the task at hand and "work together," we can do exploits. Standing alone, we don't have a chance; but if we come together and lock our shields, we can cover, encircle, and protect each other—and our nations.

4. **"AS ONE!"**[56] Power is multiplied by agreement. It is not just you, but you and your band of cohorts overlapping with other like-minded networks. As we shall see, locking shields is called "sphere overlap," and it is what the military refers to as a "force multiplier." This level of unity is not easy in the natural, but Jesus prayed *"that they may be one as we are one so that the world might know."* [57] There is a grace at work even now in nations to make this unity a reality. No prayer of Jesus will be unanswered. If Jesus prayed that we "be one," there will be a generation that will arise "as one!" If we do not do this voluntarily, the sheer force of end-time pressure in the arena will make it a necessity.

5. **"DIAMOND!"**[58] This echoes the words of Paul to the Ephesians: *"His intent was that now, through the church, the manifold wisdom of God should be made known to the rulers and authorities in the heavenly realms."*[59] The word "manifold" here is key. The Greek word for "manifold" is *polupoikilos*. This word describes something ultra-diverse, with multitudinous expressions (facets).[60] It means the many, various, ultra-diverse facets of God's glory—like a diamond. There is a facet of God's wisdom or power sufficient to solve every problem and counter every attack. The remnant working "as one" was able to counter the greater force released against them. In the coming days, God is going to use

---

55 Ephesians 6:16.

56 *Gladiator.* Dreamworks and Universal Pictures, 2000.

57 Adapted from John 17:21, 23

58 *Gladiator.* Dreamworks and Universal Pictures, 2000.

59 Ephesians 3:10 NIV.

60 "polupoikilos." (s. v.) *BibleHub,* The Lockman Foundation, 1998, https://biblehub.com/greek/4182.htm.

His Church and reveal through His body the ability of heaven to solve problems. He will use us to manifest solutions in supernatural wisdom as diverse in demonstration as the battle is diverse in its setting.

6. **"Single Column, Single Column!"**[61] In this command, Maximus divided the circle into individual columns. We keep losing battles because we do the opposite. We start off as individual groups, organizations, and silos, circling our own agendas and never coming together in collective power "as one." In terms of politics, this is the genius of the progressive left, and the Achilles heel of the conservative right. As a rule, conservatives and Christian organizations don't work together; they compete for donor dollars, mailing lists, and event attendance.

AWAKEN MAXIMUS!

The unsung heroes are about to emerge out of the ranks of the unknown. New developments are about to unfold.

God has been doing His work among us much the same way that the stones were formed for Solomon's temple. They were chiseled and hammered in the quarry so that no noise of a hammer would be present at the site where they were assembled. Many of us have been mercifully kept from public gaze as the Spirit has been patiently taking us through the breaking and forming process. This process has produced a humility and flexibility needed for the hour. The lesson is this: Before you can go on the offensive, you must learn to operate in agreement and alignment—**as one**!

The Church globally may be close to 2.2 billion souls identified as Christians; 500 million are charismatic, but that power is nothing but latent potential until it becomes activated around a common purpose and language. The activation happens wherever a Maximus steps into the equation. Leadership is a "catalytic" element that changes the status quo. God has given us secular and Christian Cyrus leaders, and in our ranks are the emerging Statesmen Evangelists, both male and female. The Zerubbabel temple builders and Haggai prophets are meeting. Nehemiahs are

---

61 *Gladiator.* Dreamworks and Universal Pictures, 2000.

surveying the walls and gates, and Ezras are opening the book to reveal the hidden things to make their meaning clear.

The Chaos Code tells us we must advance to where the gates are located. These are found in the places that shape the minds of men: politics, law, media, and academia, along with family and church. If we do nothing, the downfall of America will include the loss of freedom and inheritance we wanted to give our children. We are not destroyed by the lack of size or strength; we number nearly 90 million self-described Christians. Assume there are 50 million. We have what we need. There is only one thing we seem to lack: *"My people are destroyed for lack of knowledge."*[62] We lack understanding of this new map. We act as if we are still in the 1950s, when evangelism and church growth and revival meetings shaped culture. The church is navigating with a flat earth strategy in a digital age. The radical left redefined America—under our watch. We can break the cycle. The word of the Lord is still true: *"there is no restraint to the LORD to save by many or by few."*[63] Are you willing to be the few?

As the Chaos Code has shown us, this has happened before in church history, and the cycle is repeating today. The breakthrough happens when the people of God engage the battle differently than the way it was done in the past. The Church currently wants to start with its "single columns" of local expression, fixated on self-interest and autonomy like the individual gladiators in the arena. As the world and all of heaven watches, the reality is that our independence and autonomy from one another is no longer a match for what has come through those gates.

Somewhere there is a Maximus reading this, and the cry in their heart is **"As One!"** If you are hearing this summons let it stir you to action.

---

62 Hosea 4:6 (KJV).
63 1 Sam 14:6

EPILOGUE

I encountered *God's Chaos Code* while attempting to write a much different book. I was going to write about the 2020 election and what I saw coming. The Chaos Code unfolded in a manner that was surprising. I still included the predictions I wanted to make about 2020, but I discovered a whole lot more, and it stunned me. I discovered that you and I are not much different than our spiritual forefathers who lived through the fall of their proud nation to Babylon. It was a bitter jolt, but their captivity ended in 538 BC after a decree went forth from a king named Cyrus.

CYRUS-TRUMP AND THE BATTLE OF NATIONS

Cyrus interests me *because I predicted Donald Trump would be likened to Cyrus* a year before he became president, and indeed he has been, and declared so by officials in Israel no less. But as I went to write, I discovered other Cyrus-type rulers emerging in other nations, and in each nation this emergence revealed a similar conservative populist pushback. They were pushing back on forces destroying their culture, faith, and heritage as a nation. This is at root what the confrontation is all about in the US. But it is also what is happening in Hungary, Poland, the UK, and Brazil. The Cyrus type of ruler is raised up to resist a steadily advancing movement described by Pope Benedict XVI as a *"worldwide dictatorship of seemingly humanistic ideologies"*[1]

---

1   Katholische Nachrichten-Agentur. "Former Pope Benedict XVI sees church threatened by pseudo-humanism." *National Catholic Reporter.* 4 May 20. https://www.ncronline.org/news/quick-reads/former-pope-benedict-xvi-sees-church-threatened-pseudo-humanism

that pushes Christians and dissenters to the margins. Benedict called this a manifestation of *"the spiritual power of the Antichrist."*[2] Surprised I am quoting a pope who retired in 2013? So am I. The Chaos Code was taking me into things I had not seen before, and in the process I discovered unlikely allies.

ISRAEL—*KEY* TO THE *CODE*

As I began to write I discovered another pattern in the Code, the rise of *sheep* and *goat* nations. This is the language Jesus used in describing the status of nations when He returns. Goats are bad and sheep good. While we do not know when Jesus will return to earth, we do know where He will return. According to Zechariah, one of the prophets of the Code, Jesus will return to the Mount of Olives. Israel is the key that unlocks all the books of the Chaos Code, especially the ones that record the judgment on Israel that led to their ultimate dispersion into Babylon captivity near 600 BC—and their return to Jerusalem in 538 BC. While studying their return from Babylon, I could not help but compare it to the second regathering of Israel in 1948.

The first regathering was a big deal, but it was after only seventy years of captivity compared to the 1948 regathering after Hitler's Holocaust and nearly 2,000 years of Jewish disbursement all over the globe! It is the greatest miracle of our time. The fact that they returned to the same land, with the same faith practices and the same original, Hebrew language is one of the greatest fulfillments of prophecy in modern history. This regathering in 1948 further fulfilled Jesus's prophetic words, *"Jerusalem shall be trodden underfoot of the Gentiles until the time of the Gentiles is complete."*[3] The Jewish people retook control of Jerusalem in the Six-Day War of 1967. If the "time of the Gentiles" ended or even started to end in 1967, the time of Israel is already moving to center stage. Surely we live in a time of fulfilled prophecy, and if so, there is a promise that certain books shall be opened by divine fiat!

---

2 Jorge Solis. "Former Pope Benedict XVI Just Connected Gay Marriage With The Antichrist." *Newsweek.* 4 May 20. https://www.newsweek.com/former-pope-benedict-xvi-just-connected-gay-marriage-antichrist-1501835
3 Adapted from Luke 21:24.

UNSEALED PROPHECY

The parallels between Israel's regathering and the United States are profound because no nation in the modern era since 1948 better epitomizes the zenith of the *time of the Gentiles* than the world's greatest Gentile superpower, the United States. If you believe in the Bible, you believe there is a literal Satan, and this devil needs to bring the US down in order to advance his global agenda. Satan believes the United States and specifically, Donald Trump, must be knocked out of his way—the US must be removed. It is a restraining force.

The Chaos Code runs right up to two subjects of immense interest to the Church, namely, the rapture of the saints and the emergence of a global government with a ruler called the Antichrist. The Greek word for "antichrist" implies one situated on an opposite side. He not only assumes Christ's character but *opposes* Christ. This "man of sin," is foretold in Daniel 7:8, 25 as "the little horn speaking great words against the Most High, and thinking to change times and laws"; and the willful king who "shall exalt and magnify himself above every god, and shall speak marvelous things against the God of gods; neither shall he regard any god."[4] He shall at first be "like a lamb, while he speaks as a dragon"[5]; "coming in peaceably and by flatteries," "working deceitfully," but "his heart shall be against the holy covenant."[6]

The ***restraint*** on the Antichrist removed?

The emergence of this man cannot happen until that restraint is removed.

> *"And you know what is now restraining him, so that he may be revealed at the proper time.* **For the mystery of lawlessness is already at work, but the one who now restrains it will continue until he is taken out of the way.** *And then the lawless one will be revealed, whom the Lord Jesus will slay with the breath of His mouth."*[7]

---

4 Adapted from Daniel 7:8, 25 (KJV).
5 Adapted from Revelation 13:11.
6 Adapted from Daniel 11:21, 23, 28, 30.
7 2 Thessalonians 2 6–8 (Berean Study Bible).

A big mystery cleared up for me about this restraint and the United States when I ran into the writings of a German scholar named Hermann Olshausen (1796–1839) whose expertise was in *New Testament exegesis*. He says of this verse: "'*But the one who now restrains it will continue until he is taken out of the way.*' ... this restraining power is spoken of both in the neuter and the masculine, *both as a principle or institution, and as a person*."

In answering this question as to what holds this antichrist figure back, what exactly does keep him in check"?

Olshausen wrote:

> The power that has restrained the man of sin from his full and final development, is the moral and conservative influence of political states, the fabric of human polity as a coercive power; as "he who now letteth" refers to those who rule that polity by which the great unleashing of godlessness is kept down. The "what withholdeth" refers to the general hindrance; "he who now letteth," to the person in whom that hindrance is summed up. "*Only he who now letteth will let, until he be taken out of the way.*

I believe the collapse of America, gradual or rapid, will cause such seismic dislocations in the world's financial, military, and geopolitical spheres that it will meet the conditions of this verse for the removal of a restraining influence. It does not need to happen now.

There is more at stake in American politics than an election. An entire world order is wanting to shift, and America, if given more time, can restrain a measure of this chaos and allow the Church in emerging sheep nations to learn from the errors of the Church in America and stand with the Cyrus rulers God gives them. *This is perhaps the most important purpose of this book. America is on earth right now to buy time for other nations to get ready for the storm.* This understanding of "that which restrains" does not contradict the teaching of those who believe that the one who restrains is the Church and the Holy Spirit within her and that this verse speaks of the removal of the Spirit and the Church in the rapture. For me, the problem with this theory of interpretation is that the Holy Spirit will not be removed from earth as there are martyrs and conversions to Christ taking place right up until the end. Still, this perspective that the removal of the US and Trump at some time does not in any way negate the hope of those who see in this verse the removal of the Church in a rapture. What it does do is explain what might be happening in the world if America ceases to be a restraining economic and military force on the earth.

The Chaos Code covers a sequence that reveals what is happening in America and the world right now. It covers what to expect in the battles ahead where nations are pitted against nations. These are likely sovereign (sheep) nations resisting a one-world tyranny over the global empire. The China "One Belt, One Road" economic expansion project has sixty-two member nations to date, and they collectively represent over 30 percent of global GDP. China is on its way to being the unrestrained communist epicenter of global government and economics. This gives pause when you consider the verse "the dragon shall give its power to the beast."[8] The Code covers this.

The prophet Haggai spoke of this time, saying, *"For this is what the LORD of Hosts says: 'Once more, in a little while, I will shake the heavens and the earth … And I will shake all nations, and the desire of all nations shall come: and I will fill this house with glory,' says the LORD of hosts."*[9] God's Chaos Code reveals five specific steps for individuals, cities, and nations that will move you out of chaos and into a position that is unshakable.

I believe *God's Chaos Code* will be a constantly referenced and updated between 2020–2030 when nations align, Cyrus rulers emerge, and statesmen evangelists take their place. Those who understand the times will be wise and *"those that know their God will be strong and shall do exploits!"*[10]

Lance Wallnau
CEO Lance Learning Group
www.GodsChaosCode.com

---

8 Adapted from Revelation 13:4 (KJV).
9 Adapted from Haggai 2:6–7 (Berean Study Bible).
10 Adapted from Daniel 11:32 (KJV).

JOIN THE MOVEMENT!

The future of this nation is in the hands of the church—the people of God. That's you!

Make no mistake, God still has an unfinished assignment for America. It's time to recognize the integral role you play in the unfolding of God's prophetic purposes:

- Your individual callings have a pivotal role in God's agenda being accomplished on Earth as it is in Heaven.

- Your prayers have strategic intercessory impact in the unseen realm and impact the course of world history.

- Your voice has a direct say in the outcome of elections, policies, and the direction of nation.

WWW.GODSCHAOSCODE.COM/MOVEMENT

The Great Commission has not changed since Jesus left the earth. His vision was and is to see nations discipled.

Join me and thousands of others as we shape the course of nations one voice at a time.